THE ONE THAT
GOT AWAY

THE ONE THAT GOT AWAY

HOW I ESCAPED DEATH AT THE HANDS OF FRED AND ROSE WEST

CAROLINE ROBERTS
WITH STEPHEN RICHARDS

metro

Published by Metro Publishing,
3 Bramber Court, 2 Bramber Road,
London W14 9PB, England

www.johnblakepublishing.co.uk

www.facebook.com/Johnblakepub   facebook

twitter.com/johnblakepub   twitter

First published as *The Lost Girl* in paperback in 2005
This edition published in paperback in 2012

ISBN: 978-1-84358-952-5

British Library Cataloguing-in-Publication Data:

A catalogue record for this book is available from the British Library.

Design by www.envydesign.co.uk

Printed and bound by CPI Group (UK) Ltd, Croydon, CR0 4YY

1 3 5 7 9 10 8 6 4 2

Papers used by Metro Publishing are natural, recyclable products made from
wood grown in sustainable forests. The manufacturing processes conform to
the environmental regulations of the country of origin.

Every attempt has been made to contact the relevant copyright-holders,
but some were unobtainable. We would be grateful if the
appropriate people could contact us.

For my daughter Kelly
for giving me the will to live.

CONTENTS

INTRODUCTION

DEEP DOWN, WE all invest great hope in our families. We look to family and home to provide us with support, to help us grow, to give us love. We rely on the members of our family in a thousand ways. But what happens when a child doesn't have all that to fall back on, when the child feels let down by those closest to him or her?

I spent much of my childhood fighting against members of my family. Told from a young age that I was just a little bitch, I grew up believing it and acted accordingly. My introduction to another family – the Wests – very nearly cost me my life. I escaped from them once, only to be recaptured again and to be subjected to the most terrifying ordeal of my life. I was lucky: I managed to escape a second time. Too many others didn't.

My life went on, but the spectre of my horrendous experiences at 25 Cromwell Road continued to haunt me.

Coupled with my unhappy early years, during which I also suffered sexual abuse at the hands of strangers, I started to believe that my life was jinxed – just when I had a run of good luck, everything would come crashing down around me.

I tried to push that dark period of my life into the background for more than twenty years. But in 1994 it came screaming back on to the front page of every newspaper in the land with the arrest of Fred and Rose West. I was forced to relive my nightmare once again – this time in a court of law – and in doing so I discovered how the Wests had destroyed the lives of some of their own children.

But some good can come from even the most traumatic circumstances. To my surprise and joy, confronting the past has given me the strength to really begin to understand myself for the first time. To accept responsibility for the hurt I've brought to others and stop blaming myself for the hurt I haven't caused. To move on.

I was a lost girl for many, many years. Now I've found myself. This is how it happened.

1

TWO FACED

ON 15 OCTOBER 1928, Elizabeth Mills, my mum, was born. She was the youngest of five illegitimate children, all by different men; she never knew who her father was. Mum's mother, Lily Ann Mills, placed all but her first-born daughter Kathleen into various children's homes near Stratford-upon-Avon. Kath escaped the homes by virtue of being raised by Nanny Mills. Although my mum knew who her three older brothers were, she didn't have anything much to do with them, and when they reached the age of fifteen, they left the homes and joined the army.

After Mum left the home, she went into service for a while, then became pregnant and gave birth to a little boy, Christopher. Embarrassed by her little sister's carrying on, Kath, who was respectably married and had started a family of her own, turned her back on Mum for a few years.

Sadly, Christopher was a 'blue baby' – he had a hole in the heart and only lived for a year. Mum was unable to care for him properly as she needed to work to support herself and her baby, so she reluctantly gave him up to foster parents, whom we came to know as Ron and Nanny Munroe. They were a strict but kindly couple who fostered many children during their lifetime. Mum was allowed to visit Christopher whenever she liked and looked upon Ron and Nanny as her family.

In those days, Betty, as my mum was called, moved to Gloucester to work as a barmaid at the Black Dog pub. Whilst working in the pub, she met, and eventually married, Albert Raine whose name we took on, although he was not our father ('we' being myself and my brother Phillip, who was eighteen months older than me).

Albert was a sailor and allegedly a homosexual, so Mum informed us many years later. Our biological father, according to Mum, was an Irish roadman called Michael Mahoney whom she had started an affair with during her marriage to Albert.

Until I came along, Albert had believed Phillip, who was conceived during Mum's marriage to Albert, to be his son. I, though, looked so much like my father Michael that I couldn't be passed off as Albert's child, so he divorced my mum.

Mum told me she had never really loved Albert but she desperately wanted a child and to be in a position to raise it herself, and with Albert's support she could do it. The sexual side of their relationship was practically non-existent but she still managed to conceive and in April 1953 she gave birth to Phillip.

Phillip was fair skinned with ginger hair and freckles and he had the same pale blue eyes of Mum. He was a good baby and never any trouble to Mum or Albert. Albert would babysit while Mum worked a couple of evenings and Sunday lunchtimes at Black Dog pub.

Outwardly they were the perfect family, but in reality, the marriage was a sham.

Albert spent all the time with his old mates from the RoyalNavy, while Mum looked forward to, and enjoyed the banter and sense of humour of the 'Paddies', a gang of Irish roadmen who drank at the pub till all hours. They were a scruffy bunch in their work clothes during the week, but on the weekends they would put on their suits, shirts and tie's and the smell of tar was replaced by the smell of Brylcreem and Imperial Leather. Albert was content to play happy families believing Phillip was his son, that is, until I came along.

I was born on a wet windy Wednesday morning at Gloucester Royal Hospital in October 1955.

Mum would tell anyone who would listen, 'Caroline was such a beautiful baby with her mop of jet black hair and her big rosy cheeks. She had the most beautiful green eyes, framed by long black curly eyelashes. She was just so beautiful. When I took her back to the maternity ward that morning all the other mums and nurses couldn't believe she was a newborn. She looked three months old she was so bonny.'

I used to cringe when mum bragged about me, her beautiful daughter. She made me sound like Snow White.

I didn't look anything like Mum or Albert but I did bear an uncanny resemblance to one of the Irish roadmen, Michael Mahoney.

Albert already suspected Mum was having an affair and seeing me just confirmed it for him. That in turn put doubt in his mind about Phillip being his son. The farce of a marriage was over and Mum took eighteen month old Phillip and me, a babe in arms, and left Albert.

We moved in to Quedgely Court, a big mansion-type house on the south side of Gloucester that had been converted into bedsits, and lived there for a couple of years. I remember it well, even though I was just a toddler at the time. We lived there until Mum got behind with the rent and then we had to leave.

When I was three years old, Mum took a job as a house-keeper to a farmer and his two sons on a farm in Painswick. Sadly the farmer had lost his wife and needed Mum to help out with the day-to-day housekeeping chores.

I loved living on the farm, chasing the ducks, milking the goats, plucking chickens and riding my pedal car down the long, steep drive. I missed my dad coming round to tuck me in to bed as he did at Quedgely Court, but he still took us out on the weekends for a ride around the country lanes – Mum and Dad on the motorbike, Phillip and me in the sidecar. Ever since then, I have always had a fascination for motorbikes and the men that ride them. Maybe through them, in a strange way, I feel I'm with my dad again.

I don't know why, but we left the farm and ended up staying with Michael, my dad, in his flat in Matson on the outskirts of Gloucester. He usually shared the flat with his workmates, but at the time they had just returned to Ireland for a couple of months, so there was room for us.

I liked being with my dad; he was a kind and religious man,

a devout Catholic. He had crucifixes hanging on the wall and a beautiful painting of Mary and the baby Jesus. I always felt that Mary's eyes were staring at me, watching me, especially after Dad told me he would know if I had been a naughty girl because Mary would tell him!

Of course, I tried to be good, but it wasn't long before I got into trouble. I stole a pile of shillings off the kitchen shelf and attempted to spend them at the grocery van that called at the council estate. The 'Van man', as I knew him, dobbed me in it, and it was after this that Dad gave me my first and last scolding. Even though he didn't smack me, his disappointment in me hurt me more than any of the beatings I was to suffer later on in my life.

Soon afterwards, we had to leave the flat and moved in with friends of Mum and Dad's, Jim and Joan Brady. The Brady family lived in a three-bedroom flat on the same estate; they had five children of their own at the time, and the stay was only meant to be short-term – a stop-gap. Mum was desperate to find us somewhere to live. She had told friends that she would not give up her children; she would never allow us to go into a children's home – never!

In the spring of 1960, my mum met Alfred William Harris, a coalminer from Cinderford, a small town in the Forest of Dean, through mutual friends. Within six weeks of meeting him, Mum married Alfred (Alf), the man who was to become my stepfather. We were homeless and Alf was recently widowed, so it was more a marriage of convenience than a marriage of love, though I'm sure they grew to love each other over the years.

Four older stepchildren – Ray, Josey, Keith and Chris – were now part of my family. Then there was me – by now five years old – and Phillip. But we weren't to be the last of the children by far! My first sister, Suzanne (later called Sue), was soon born and eighteen months later twins Angela and Adrian arrived. Shortly after that, Mum lost a set of twins in an ectopic pregnancy, but became pregnant again straight away and successfully gave birth to two more twins, Richard and Robert.

While Mum was heavily pregnant with the twin boys, Josephine, who was by this time seventeen, got married to her fiancé John. They decided to go on a boating honeymoon and invited Ray and his fiancée Betty as well as our cousin Rose and her new husband John. (Strange coincidence but our Rose's maiden name was West and John's nickname was Fred, they were known as Fred and Rose West but that's where the familiarity ends.) One night after a few beers, Ray went up on deck alone and never returned, his body was washed up three days later, he was just nineteen.

In the short time Ray had lived with us, he had made my life a living hell. He would call me 'the spoilt brat' – and this when I was only nine years old! He caused plenty of arguments between my mum and Alf, and he seemed to enjoy hurting me, both physically and mentally. When our parents were out, he would make me sit still on a chair and, if I moved or spoke, he would hit me around the face. Even when I had a bad nosebleed, which I was prone to, he would hit me for making a mess, and call me a 'dirty bitch'. He knew I had a weak stomach, so he would tell me he had spat in my porridge or put bogeys in it; he'd do anything to upset me and was always spoiling for any reason to take it out on me. When I complained, I'd get a telling-off or a smack for making a fuss.

The worst thing Ray did was to tell me over the Sunday roast that I was eating my pet rabbit Snowy, which had, I thought, escaped from his hutch the day before. As it happens, it was true. I was so upset that I cried and ranted at Alf for being a murderer and swore that I would never eat rabbit again. After that, Alf started hitting me about and picking on me. There was one grim consolation though: Ray had left for good, he was dead and he wasn't coming back.

I always made matters worse by telling Alf, 'You're not my dad. My dad will come and take me away to live with him, and I don't have to do as you tell me!' Well, my high hopes of a reunion with my real father were soon dashed: Alf stopped my father, Michael, from seeing me. I was six years old at the time and believed that they had a falling-out over money. Years later, I was to find out the truth.

We were a big family on a low income and money was tight. An accident at work had put a premature end to Alf's career. (Ironically, a year or so later the coalmine where Alf had his accident was shut down.) With so many of us in the house, personal space was unheard of – both in the flat we first moved into and, eventually, in the three-bedroom council house that we moved to when I was eleven years old. The only room in the house that you had to yourself was the bathroom, which had a lock on the door. Thank God we had a down-stairs toilet too.

No longer the baby of the family, I gradually started to feel rejected. I would play up to get my busy mother's attention. I longed for the feeling of being loved and protected by my older siblings and loved and looked up to by my younger siblings, yet I always felt like an outcast. I was desperate for love and affection and, being the middle child in a family of ten children, I had to fight to get the attention I craved. I would do anything to be the centre of attention at home, even if it meant getting a good hiding. Any attention was better than none at all.

The only person whom I felt ever truly loved me was my mum. I was her special child, because I was my father's daughter, and my father was the only man she had ever loved. Mum, too, had been the outcast in her family, as had her mother before her, so maybe that was another reason why she loved me – she understood me better than anyone else. I believe that my mother saw herself mirrored in me when I was young, and could see the hurt I was feeling from being rejected. My mother shielded the blows that life threw at me, always trying to cushion the physical and emotional knocks. When someone hurt me, my mother would worry and get upset. Out of my love for her, I would never let her know just how bad I was feeling.

2

WEARING 'MY HAPPY FACE'

I ALWAYS THOUGHT of myself as being the unluckiest girl I knew. I was, I believed, a 'jinx'. Nothing much good happened to me, and if anything bad were going to happen to anyone … it would happen to me! Life had been a bitch to me and I grew up expecting that nothing good would come of me or my life.

I was used to being let down and feeling unwanted. I knew how it felt to be disliked by those who were supposed to love me; they didn't mean to make me feel bad about myself, but that's what happened.

I felt I had two different faces, two separate personalities. Each of my personalities was at odds with the other. I was a rebel, a spoilt brat and a little show-off. Many times, my stepfather Alf would rebuke my behaviour with the line, 'You can sit down now, Caroline, we've all seen you.'

I was the troublemaker of the family, the argumentative one

who answered back, the one who never did as she was asked first time – it was always 'In a minute' with me. I pushed my luck, constantly defying my parents and annoying my older siblings. From 'little bitch' I progressed to 'dirty little bitch'. I was used to the name-calling. It had started when I was four years old and continued right up into my twenties – and that was just in the place I called home.

My other personality was the 'shy girl' – the little girl who would sit for hours on her own in a field full of horses, dreaming of owning one some day. I would make bridles out of rope, straddle a kitchen chair and have my imaginary mount gallop off. I pretended it was my pony. I had a huge appetite for reading books on how to care for a pony and how to ride. I would see other kids riding their real ponies at the gymkhana, hoping one of them would take pity on me and offer me a ride, but they never did.

All I dreamed and longed for was a pony of my own and of being with my real dad again. My dad had told me how he had been raised on a farm in Ireland and went on to say that Grandma had a pony and how she would love me to be there with her and my dad.

All of this, though, was just a dream; Grandma's farm and the pony existed for me but, years later, I was to find out that I didn't exist for them – at least not for Grandma, nor anyone in my dad's family. The dad I had hero-worshipped and adored had given me up without a fight when I was four years old. As a devout Catholic, he was ashamed of me, the bastard he had fathered. I was the dark secret he took to his grave.

When I was in my teens, people outside the family and the

home saw me as a pretty, bubbly and friendly girl who liked the boys – a little too much at times – and the boys certainly seemed to like me too. I was well mannered and helpful, always available to babysit, always kind and polite, with a good sense of humour and a smile on my face. I would put the smiles on to hide the fact that more often than not I would just have had my head smashed against the wall for answering back.

I called this face my 'happy face'; I used it many times, to mask my tears and my pain. I didn't want other people to be embarrassed at my expense; I didn't want them to know why I had been given a beating. I didn't want them to know what a horrible young girl I could be. I needed them to like me and I needed their approval. I could also use this 'happy face' to deflect the pain caused by the scathing words and remarks that people would use against me.

When one of my brothers, or my stepfather, said or did anything that hurt my feelings, I would lock it away. I learned how to hide my feelings of hurt with displays of bravado and sarcasm – or a big smile. If someone wanted to hurt me, I would beam a huge smile at him or her, just to be annoying; it always did the trick.

Sometimes, I wouldn't be able to control my temper and I would lash out verbally and, sometimes, physically, but only towards those who knew me best – my family, especially Alf and Phillip and later my boyfriends. To them I could be a bitch, but in my twisted little mind I was just surviving.

I'd had so many bad things happen to me that I knew it would only be a matter of time before I ended up dead. I had many, many dreams about my demise. Vivid dreams that I thought were most probably premonitions of what was to come. I kept these dreams to myself. Very often, I dreamed of my death at the hands of some madman – or woman. I knew by experience that women were not to be trusted any more than men when it came to me. In my dreams, I knew how it felt to be strangled, gasping for breath, my tongue jutting out between my blue lips, my eyes bulging and bloodshot. I also knew what it felt like to have a knife stab me through the stomach – it didn't seem to hurt that much, though it made me feel sick as my stomach gurgled and churned, but when the knife pierced my chest it hurt like hell! I would be fighting for breath as though I was drowning in my own blood; this panic feeling always woke me with a start and I would go to pieces.

I knew I would be famous one day, but it wasn't until I was seventeen years old that I began to keep a diary so someone could write a book about my poor, sad life, when (I predicted) I died of unnatural causes. Yes, I thought, it would come in very handy when my body was found dead and buried under the paving stones of Gloucester.

3

THE CURSE OF BEING ATTRACTIVE

MUM TRIED TO give me confidence by telling me, often, what an attractive girl I was, and when I complained of having no nice clothes to wear she would say, 'Caroline, you could be wearing a sack and you'd still stand out and look beautiful.' I found that being attractive had its downside though, as it meant that I attracted all sorts of people – including the perverts and weirdos. I learned to my cost that I was attractive to paedophiles as a child. I suppose being indecently assaulted when I was thirteen years old should have warned me that there were some weird and dangerous men out there.

A man had followed me into the public toilets in Gloucester Park; I was waiting while my friend used the cubicle first. Initially, I thought he had come in by mistake and I had started to tell him that the 'Gents' was around the other side of the building. He kept coming towards me with a blank look on his face. I backed away from him until the cold tiled wall pressed up against my back and stopped my escape. He grabbed at me. I struggled to get away as he forced his hands down my knickers. I tried to scream, but all that came out was a weird gurgling noise. I grabbed at his fingers, trying to pull them away, but he was too strong for me. I heard a cracking sound and was sure I must have broken his finger, but still he wouldn't let go.

My friend Dawn came out of the toilet to see me squatting down with this elderly man bent over me. Dawn was only eleven, and tiny for her age, but even so she jumped on his back and tried to get him off me; he was too strong for both of us though. Dawn ran out and raised the alarm; she returned with two men, who finally dragged the old man off me. I was so relieved when I was rescued that I started giggling uncontrollably, a mixture of relief and embarrassment.

When the police came for him, the old man looked a shadow of the brutal figure that had just attacked me. What they saw was a sad and pathetic flat-capped figure who cried in front of the crowd of onlookers that had gathered to see what was going on. Among the crowd was a group of young men, all calling out to the police, 'Let the poor bugger go.' Maybe it was because of the fact that I didn't look harmed by the attack that they took pity on the man and made me feel like it was *I* who had done something wrong, not him!

When the police took me home to our house, all the neighbours came out to their gates or peered out from behind their curtains as I was led by the arm to our front door. Alf came to the front door with a look of thunder in his eyes. As if I had been caught shoplifting, he seethed, 'What's she been up to now?' He didn't like the police being at his door, whatever the reason. Even when he was told what had happened to me, he still didn't appear to be concerned about the attack or what effect it would have on me. Mum was the one who sat me down and asked if I was all right.

The old man was charged and the police told Alf that the man had previous form for this sort of thing, that he had attacked several schoolgirls throughout his life and was well known to the police. This put a stop to Alf thinking I was just making a fuss, and not just making it all up to get some attention. Nevertheless, I felt he still thought that, somehow, I had asked for it.

What happened in Gloucester Park that day changed my life and although I was hardened on the outside my dreams and nightmares told the real story of how vulnerable I really felt. I resigned myself to the fact that I would die at an early age, after a sexual assault or even, possibly, rape, which would be followed by murder. From then on, rather than try to save myself and watch out for the dangers in life, I went on a mission of self-destruction, as if I knew I couldn't escape my destiny.

For a while after the park attack, I went through a depression caused by what had happened to me. At the time, I didn't understand what was wrong with me. I just felt sad all the time and became quiet. Most of my friends were trying to make themselves look older and attractive, but I went back to wearing my hair in plaits and wearing longer skirts.

At the age of thirteen, I was less physically developed than most of my crowd, and decided that perhaps this was for the best as it would stop men looking at me or touching me, as the old man had. I was left with deep-seated mental scars and whenever an old man, particularly if he was wearing a flat cap, came towards me I would cross the road to avoid him.

My mum noticed these changes within me. One day she sat me down and asked me how I was. For once, as I choked back the tears, I told her how I felt the old man had fancied me because I was pretty and was dressed in a short dress. And as the tears came in torrents, I gushed, 'He must have thought I was a prostitute, Mum!'

I went on to tell Mum that I had the feeling that this sort of sexual attack had happened to me before but couldn't remember it properly; it was like déjà vu. She looked at me and started to cry too, then she told me something that shocked me: 'It did happen to you before, but you were only six years old. I didn't think you would remember it.'

My mother went on to tell me how she and Alf had left me with an elderly family friend while they went Christmas shopping. I recalled that the elderly man was a nice old gent, always cuddling me and giving me presents; it was around the time when my real dad had stopped seeing me. Mum told me how she and Alf had walked in to find the old man touching me up, and how Alf got really angry and dragged me out of the old man's house, leaving him crying.

My mum also told me that she was angry with Alf for not doing something about it and because of what he had said – 'The old man can't be held responsible for what he has done, he's not right in the head.' Mum didn't realise it, but what she was really telling me was that Alf thought if the old man wasn't responsible for the sexual assault then it must have been my fault. From then on, I knew I was bad and no matter what happened to me – because I was a bad girl, a dirty girl – I deserved what I got.

This made things even harder for me at home because I felt Alf hated the sight of me. To him I was a spoilt brat who needed to be disciplined, and was – regularly. Once, he hit my head so violently into a wall that it perforated my eardrum. And if he hated me, then I hated him. I promised myself that when I left school I would leave home and get a live-in job at a hotel or as a children's nanny – anything to get away from the people who made me feel bad about myself.

My brother Phillip grew to hate me more as I got older, because as a child I was a troublemaker who disrupted family life. As a teenager, I was what Phillip considered to be a slut. He hated the fact that when I was fifteen years old, he would overhear his friends down the pub refer to me as 'Jailbait of the year'. I was an embarrassment to him.

My stepbrother Ray, meanwhile, had hated my mum for taking the place of his real mum who had died in her thirties. So he took it out on me too.

Then there was that nice old man who had showed me affection at the age of six … but who, at the same time, was sexually abusing me. They had all let me down; they were supposed to care for me, love me and protect me. Not one had stayed; they had all left me.

Some of them hurt me physically and mentally and some hurt me by their keenly felt absence. I grew used to being let down by those around me, but it didn't hurt quite so much as the hurt I felt from the absence of my real father during those childhood days.

4

JAILBAIT

I WAS POPULAR amongst my classmates, getting on well with both the girls and boys. I was a middle-of-the-road student, but I knew I would never manage to get through my exams – I lacked concentration and confidence. In class, I would never raise my hand to answer a question just in case I got it wrong, although a lot of the time I knew the correct answer. I always appeared happy and confident, but inside I was terribly shy. My bravado and bluff were my way of coping with it.

At fifteen years of age, I was pretty. My eyes were my best feature, like my dad's. They were a greeny grey in colour with thick black curly eyelashes. My second best feature was my hair, which was long, dark and shiny. I was only 5ft 2in tall and of slender build; although I had developed boobs, they weren't very big, but I was in proportion. My worst feature, I thought, were my thighs; I always thought they looked fat, though no one else thought they did. I was a late developer and envied the girls who already had boobs, pubic hair and periods. My periods came along when I was fifteen and a half years old.

My sister Sue and I were unfortunate in that we were both knock-kneed. We cost our mum a fortune in shoes, as we always wore the heels down fast. We were sent to a clinic to be trained how to walk properly – backs straight and chests out. I was already walking this way before my boobs developed, but when they did eventually arrive I looked like I was deliberately trying to stick my chest out, and this got me plenty of leg-pulling from the boys, and sarcastic remarks from the girls.

Alf was well aware of my new assets and seemed to come down even harder on me, nagging me about what I wore, where I went, with whom I went out and what time I got in. We seemed to spend all of our time arguing. Looking back, I can see why.

As I blossomed into a young woman, I attracted young men who were several years older than myself. I didn't know how to deal with the attention they lavished on me. I could feel their eyes on me as I walked home from school in my navy uniform, my skirt rolled up at the waistband, until I reached the turning into our cul-de-sac. I enjoyed the attention and flattery; it made me feel good about myself.

I lost my virginity at fifteen. It wasn't as I had imagined it would be – it was uncomfortable and awkward. I stayed with my first lover for a year, but my jealousy ruined everything, as it would do so often in the years to come.

All I wanted was to be loved, but I found that the men

couldn't make do with just a kiss and cuddle. They would call me a tease and make me feel bad about myself, or I would feel like a silly little girl and give in to their desires, either to keep them or so they would go away, as they wouldn't take 'no' for an answer.

Girls, jealous because their boyfriends looked at me, bullied me. My stepfather bullied me. My brother Phillip would call me names and pretend to throw up as I walked past him when we were out at the local discos, where I danced provocatively. I was used to being put down by Phillip. I pretended I didn't care what he thought of me, but it did hurt my feelings. I wanted us to be close, like other friends of mine; they got on well with their brothers. I refused to let him or anyone else see that they had succeeded in hurting me; I would put on my 'happy face' to cover the pain I really felt inside.

I've used my 'happy face' throughout my life, on many occasions; it became my friend. It protected my pride and my feelings; it was a protective barrier I put up around myself. No one was allowed to penetrate that barrier. And, as the years went by, it made me appear confident, when really I felt like a second-class citizen. It was a necessity, as I found I couldn't talk about my real feelings to anyone. Not to my mum, who would have been too affected by what I was going through. And not to my friends – they were used to me being the life and soul of the party, the bubbly girl with the wicked sense of humour. They wouldn't have believed how inferior I felt compared to them.

At sixteen years of age, I left home and was living in Southsea, Portsmouth, with my neighbour and friend from Cinderford,

Doreen. I ended up getting thrown out by Doreen's sister, Dee, whom we were staying with, because she had grounded us for letting two sailors stay the night while she was away. I had defied her and left when she tried to stop me seeing my sailor boyfriend of the time, Steve Riddall.

After a short spell in a grotty bedsit, the police came round to tell me that Alf had suffered a heart attack and my mother wanted me home. I hitchhiked home immediately. Alf looked older and frailer than I remembered him. I tried to be nice to him, scared that if I made him angry again he would die. I was glad to be back home again, and tried my best to get on with the rest of the family, helping Mum around the house, cooking the tea for everyone and looking after Alf, who was still recovering from his heart attack. I kept busy, being helpful. For once, I felt Alf appreciated that I was trying to please him.

5

25 CROMWELL STREET

I FIRST MET Fred and Rose West in early September 1972. I had been hitchhiking back from Tewkesbury after seeing my boyfriend Tony, whom I had met at the annual Tewkesbury Ham Fair. We had been seeing each other for two months by then. I was nearly seventeen years old; he was six months younger than me, but seemed really mature for his age.

Tony was a skinhead and well respected by the older boys in the town. The relationship was still in its early days and we weren't lovers. In fact, Tony was such a cool dude that I wasn't really sure where I stood with him, but I was hoping it would become a long-term relationship.

I was used to hitchhiking everywhere – lots of young girls did it – and with Tony not driving yet, it was easier for me to travel to him. Most of the time I took a friend with me and we would hang around the town with Tony and his mate Rob.

Sometimes we would go to discos in the town hall or sit in the café drinking Coke and chatting. Then, at about 10.30pm, I would stand opposite the Gupshil Manor, on the edge of town, and say good night.

Tony would go back to his lodgings, leaving me to get myself a lift home to Cinderford. The journey home was some twenty-five miles, which I usually made in two lifts. The first lift took me the ten miles to Gloucester, and then I'd get another lift from the Westgate Bridge, which was fifteen miles to Cinderford.

That night in September 1972, I remember noticing the grey-coloured Ford Popular going in the opposite direction just minutes before it pulled up alongside me. At first I was a little worried in case two men were inside, but when I saw there was a girl in the passenger seat I relaxed.

The girl rolled down the window and asked me where I was going. As I bent down to tell her, I noticed that the driver was leaning over, looking at me. He looked quite scruffy and much older than the girl who, I guessed, was my age. They offered me a lift and, feeling it was a safe ride, I accepted. The girl got out and lifted her seat so I could get into the rear seat of the two-door car.

Straight away, they started chatting and telling me their names: Fred and Rose West. I was surprised that they were married; I wouldn't have fancied someone like him, and she was pretty. I felt she could have done a lot better for herself, but they seemed happy and he was quite charming, in a roguish kind of way.

During the first part of the journey they questioned me a lot, asking about where I had been and who with, and did I have a job. I told them that I had been away to Portsmouth for six months and that I had to come back because my stepfather had suffered a heart attack, and was very ill though he had pulled through.

I explained to them that Alf was the reason I had gone away in the first place. I told them that we had never got on and that I had felt he was always on my case, always finding fault with me. As soon as he became ill, I revealed, I had wanted to get to him, hoping we would get on better but we had soon started arguing again and things were back to being tense at home, so I spent most of my time out of the house avoiding him. I mentioned to Fred and Rose that Alf had started nagging me because I didn't have a job and how he called he me lazy, saying I would never make anything of myself, and would most probably end up pregnant and living off the government. I had looked for a job, but I felt I was not capable of getting anything decent.

After I had finished explaining this to the pair of them, they both looked each other in the eye and then, at the same time, both said, 'We need a nanny to look after our three daughters.'

They went on to tell me that they lived in a big house in Cromwell Street, Gloucester, and that if I wanted the job I could move in with them. They offered me £8 a week plus free board and lodgings.

I told them I would have to talk to my mum about it first, and that she would want to meet them first before anything could be decided. They said they would be happy to meet my parents and with that they drove me all the way home so that they would know where I lived and said that they would come back on the Sunday afternoon to meet my parents. I wasn't sure how my mum would react to Fred, as he was quite rough looking. I hoped he would make the effort to look tidier when he came round, though as it turned out he didn't.

When they arrived, after dinner on the Sunday, they had the three girls with them; I instantly fell in love with them, especially little Heather. I could tell from the look on Mum's face that she was not impressed by Fred's appearance. He noticed it too, and quickly apologised for having to come in his working clothes. He said he was working all hours, and that was why Rose needed some help around the house and with the demanding job of looking after the children. Rose left most of the talking to Fred, who reassured my mum that he would look after me and keep a fatherly eye on me. Meanwhile, Rose chatted to my younger brothers and sisters.

Alf popped into the room just once while they were there. He looked Fred up and down, then he looked at Rose, who gave him a smile. He smiled back and said, 'Make sure she doesn't run wild,' then went back out to his shed and his DIY.

The next day, I moved into 25 Cromwell Street, a three-storey townhouse just 300 yards from the park that had held bad memories for me; the park that I would not be taking the children to during my time at their home. It didn't take me long to get acquainted with the West household and to form my own opinions about them all.

At 31 years of age, Fred West was a big man trapped in a little man's body. He clearly thought of himself as a gynaecologist and Warren Beatty lookalike all rolled into one; the surgeon and the stud. The reality was that he worked in a factory, doing the occasional odd job on the side. This budding 'surgeon' bragged that he had performed abortions for girls in trouble; according to him, they were usually so grateful to him that they would offer themselves to him for his sexual pleasures as soon as the foetus was removed. 'I've had thousands of women,' he told me; they would, he claimed, fall at his feet.

Fred West's incessant bragging was at best annoying and at worst sickening. According to him, he was God's gift to women. 'Once you'd been with Freddie, you wouldn't go anywhere else,' he'd say. How true this was to prove.

In reality, Fred West was a short little man with piercing blue eyes, a flat, wonky nose and thick lips that hid a gap in his front teeth. Not at all attractive. His mop of hair was gypsy-like – dark and curly. All he needed was a scarf around his head and one of those big loop earrings in his ear and he would have been transformed into Gypsy Rose Lee. He was never tidy, his favourite outfit being jeans, a check shirt and a donkey jacket. I couldn't see how anyone would find him attractive, except perhaps someone simple or needy.

At nineteen years of age, the words that best described Rose would be 'simple-minded'. In spite of this, she was quite a pretty girl, two years older than me, with dark wavy hair and big brown doe eyes. Rose had a whiny, drippy way of talking that, at times, I found very grating, but not half as irritating as when she yelled at her little ones. That high-pitched scream emitted by Rose made me wince. Her ear-bursting howls would stun me into silence, much as it did the eldest child in their home, eight-year-old Anna-Marie. (Later to rename herself Anne-Marie.) While two-year-old Heather and four-month-old May (later changed to Mae) would also instantly shut up at the sound of that scream, this only worked on them for a minute or two; they were not old enough yet to be smacked around the head, as Anna-Marie was.

Anna-Marie was Fred's daughter from a previous marriage. Heather and May were Fred and Rose's daughters. I was told by Anna-Marie that she had a big sister called Charmaine who had 'gone away', back to Scotland with her mother; Fred's first wife, Rena, was a Scottish lass. Fred told me that he wouldn't let Rena take Anna-Marie with her because she was not a 'fit mother'. As for Charmaine, she was of mixed heritage, but that was a different story. Fred was not Charmaine's father; her biological father was of Asian origin.

Anna-Marie looked like a pretty version of her father, but that was where the likeness ended. Unlike her father, she was quiet and shy, a child who, to me, always looked sad. I felt quite sorry for her as she worked around the house, fetching and carrying like a little skivvy. If she sulked, she got yelled at or caught a back-hander off Rose, who obviously cared more for her own daughters; she looked on Anna-Marie as her slave.

When Anna-Marie cried, she cried quietly to herself for fear of further punishment at Rose's hands. Fred, on the other hand, never smacked her; sometimes he would wink at her, when Rose wasn't looking, as if to reassure her that she would be OK.

I didn't like or approve of the way Rose sometimes behaved towards Anna, and I often got Anna to do something to help me around the house so as to get her away from Rose if she was in a bad mood, though Rose was always nice to me. Rose thought I was very pretty and she loved my hair, which she often played with as we sat watching TV. She thought I had beautiful eyes too and often complimented me on my looks. We became friends and I liked her – until I got to know the real Rose and saw her dark side.

It was because of the children that I ended up living with this odd couple – that and a schoolgirl dream of being a 'nanny'. That dream didn't quite match the scenario of living with the Wests in Cromwell Street though. My dream included a rich family, with whom I would travel the world. I'd have my own big room with a TV and a record player, and the children would be beautiful and behave like angels.

With the Wests, I got only one part of my dream – the children were indeed little angels. Two decades later, I would find out, along with the rest of the world, that they were 'angels born out of demons'.

I had been disappointed when I found out I would not be getting my own bedroom at Cromwell Street; instead, I would be sharing with Anna-Marie on the first floor, in the back bedroom. I was surprised that some of the rooms upstairs were actually rented out as bedsits, and even more taken aback to find that the some of the lodgers were a group of male hippies.

One of the lodgers, Ben, was just a year older than me; he was tall and handsome with long brown hair – he was gorgeous! The first time I saw Ben I developed a crush on him. One day Ben invited me up to his room. I wasn't used to smoking cannabis, but as we lay on the floor chatting I didn't want to appear immature, so I smoked a joint with him and listened to music. He kissed me and I responded, feeling relaxed by the infusion of drugs, and we ended up having sex. Afterwards I fell asleep on the floor in his arms.

Later I woke to find someone, an occasional visitor to the house, climbing on top of me. I was still lying on the floor and this man was attempting to have intercourse with me! I told him to get off and leave me alone. He became verbally abusive towards me. Fortunately Ben woke up and told the man to leave me alone.

I felt so ashamed of myself as I crept back into my room and quietly cried myself to sleep. Somehow Fred and Rose got to know about what had happened that night and tried to talk to me about it, but it was something I wanted to forget.

Fred suggested that Tony, my boyfriend, should stay once a week, the night before he had college. It would save him having to ride his pushbike from Tewkesbury to Gloucester early in the morning and we would get some time to ourselves. On these nights, Tony helped me with the children while Fred and Rose went out, either for a drink or to do a bit of work on the side, with Rose labouring for her husband. Tony and I became once-a-week lovers, but my guilt about what had happened with the lodgers had left deep-seated emotional scars and made me feel cheap. Sex with Tony became a chore; I just went through the motions when it should have been something special.

I had one more lover while I was living at Cromwell Street, and this time it was the Wests who had fixed it up. An old flame from Portsmouth, whom had I continued writing to, wrote saying he would like to visit me on my seventeenth birthday. The old flame was Steve Riddall. He was quite snobby and loved himself; I used to fancy him like mad. I didn't expect him to show up – he never had before – so when he arrived at Cromwell Street, I was gobsmacked.

Fred and Rose tried to chat to Steve, but I could see he was looking down his nose at them, so I suggested we went out for a drink on our own. ('What are you doing living with those two weirdos?' he asked me when we were out of the house.) When we got back, Rose told me, 'You can use our room tonight, I've changed the bedding for you.'

That night I nervously got into bed still wearing my undies and a T-shirt, not wanting Steve to see my body. Within minutes he had them off and was making love to me … properly. Steve was a skilled lover with plenty of experience. That night I had my first ever orgasm. He laughed at me when I told him 'something strange has happened to me'. 'I feel all funny,' I said. 'My legs have gone stiff and a strange, but nice, feeling has come over me and my heart's thumping so much I think I'm having a heart attack.'

'That's an orgasm,' he told me, still laughing.

Next morning, I saw Steve off at the train station. I never saw him again, though we kept in touch by letter for another year until he stopped replying.

When I got back to the house, Rose asked me how it went with Steve. I told her about my orgasm and how I had never really enjoyed sex before, but that now I knew what all the fuss was about, now I understood why she enjoyed it so much. I didn't mind telling Rose about it – it was girlie talk – but I was annoyed when, later that day, I discovered that she had told Fred everything I had told her during our chat. He used to make everything to do with sex seem smutty, when in my mind it had been a beautiful experience.

Living in the West household was beginning to get me down. I soon realised that Steve was right; they were a weird lot after all!

One night, a tall, buxom blonde girl named Dee came to the house and, as I opened the door to her, she started shouting and swearing at me, accusing me of stealing her babysitting job. Fred came to the door and led her into their bedroom, trying to calm her down, and Rose followed. After ten minutes, all three of them came into the living room and Dee apologised to me.

Rose made a cup of tea and they sat around laughing and joking with Dee, who obviously knew them well. Dee asked me if I would like to go out with her that night to the Jamaican Club. Her boyfriend was in a reggae band and they were rehearsing there. At first I wasn't sure I wanted to go. I was wary of black men – the only ones I had spoken to were the two that regularly visited the house once or twice a week and, even then, I hardly spoke to them. One of the visiting black men was old and went off somewhere with Rose as soon as he arrived. The other of the two was young and always had a silly grin on his face, but seemed quite nice. His name was Roy and I used to make him a cup of tea while he waited to see Rose, whom I innocently believed was a masseuse at that time. They were both friends of Fred's so I never suspected that they were having affairs with Rose in her home, with her husband around.

That night, Fred and Rose both urged me to go out with Dee to the club and, against my better judgement, I took Dee up on her offer. I found Dee to be very loud and embarrassing. Every other word that she spoke was an expletive – but who was I to look down on her after my behaviour? Since moving in with the Wests, I had taken on some new lovers and discovered the satisfaction of an orgasm.

When we got to the club, the band were already packing their equipment away out the back. There were about seven of them altogether, including the one that Dee pointed out to me as her boyfriend. I sat nervously at the bar next to an old man; he tried to make conversation with me. Dee went outside to see her boyfriend and was gone for ages. I tried to be polite and talk to this old-timer, but I couldn't understand much of what he was saying in his strong Jamaican accent.

One of the boys came up to me and asked me to go outside too, but something didn't feel quite right about him, or the others, so I said, 'No, it's OK, I'll wait here for Dee.'

After a while, Dee came back in. Her hair was messed up and her clothes were dishevelled.

I left the club and as soon as I got out of the door my instincts told me to run! I knew that I wasn't safe there. As I ran, I heard some of the boys shouting at me to come back. I looked around and they all started running after me. I darted off and ran as fast as I could. My lungs were on fire from the exertion and my eyes were bursting with the fear. By the time I could see 25 Cromwell Street, only one of the black men was still chasing me. As I hit the door of the Wests' home, he gave up, turned around and walked off back in the direction of the club.

I told Fred and Rose about it, expecting them to go to the club to see if Dee was all right, but they seemed to think it was funny. All Fred wanted to know was how many men there had been. I went to bed feeling lucky that I had escaped and got in safely.

The next day, while Fred was at work and Rose was out shopping, Dee called round. She told me how she had got to know Fred when he came to her workplace for DIY materials. Fred had invited her and her Jamaican boyfriend back to the house for some supper.

Dee asked, 'Has Rose tried it on with you yet?'

'No! She hasn't,' I retorted with a tone of indignity to my voice.

'She will,' Dee predicted, as she winked at me.

I replied, 'Rose has never tried it on with me, and if she does I'd be out of here.'

'Rose likes women, you know. She'll have you in bed before long,' Dee said.

It was Dee that first made me suspicious about Rose and Fred, but I think by then I already thought they had a strange sort of marriage, what with Rose giving massages and Fred going with her.

After Dee's revelations, I started to look at all the visitors in a different light – the old Polish guy they had bought the house from, the old black man, even nice Roy no longer seemed so nice. In my mind's eye, I started to look upon Fred's brother, John West, who called around every teatime, with suspicion too. I began to watch him out of the corner of my eye as he chatted to Fred at the kitchen table, and many a time I caught him looking me up and down. John was quiet, not like Fred, but I remember my mum telling me, 'The quiet ones are always the worst.'

I started to think of the times Rose had come into the bathroom while I was bathing. She always had an excuse, like needing the baby soap or that she was dying for a pee. She always stayed for a minute or two, talking to me. I had found it highly embarrassing but, naively, I never thought she was just coming in to look at my body.

From then on, I would put something in front of the door so I'd have time to get out and grab a towel before she came in. I began to be suspicious of everyone in that house, and realised it was not a safe place at all for a young girl to be. I thought of the smutty conversations that went on between them all and realised they were all bonded together in an unhealthy way.

Then, one day, Fred started talking about sex to me again. This time he revealed to me, 'Anna's not a virgin, you know!'

'What do you mean, she's not a virgin?' I replied accusingly.

I looked across at little Anna-Marie, who was sat quietly watching television, and caught her darting a look at her father, then to me. Then she lowered her eyes back at the television screen.

Surprised by the venom in my tone, Fred quickly added, 'Oh, the saddle came off her bike and she sat down on the bar and it went up inside her. She was messed up for a while, but at least she'll not have any pain now when she has sex.'

I looked at Anna again and saw that she was blushing. That told me she was most probably being sexually abused – by her own father. As if Fred had read my thoughts, he changed the subject and got on to the subject of my sex life and abortions again, telling me that if I got pregnant he would 'sort me out' – he would abort the baby and save me having my stepfather finding out what a naughty girl I was. He went on to say that Tony needn't know anything about it, especially as it might not be his baby, the way I'd been bed-hopping recently.

Winking at me, he said, 'It will be our little secret.'

What he really meant was, 'You keep my secret and I'll keep yours.' In other words, it was blackmail. Fred had sussed me out. He knew I wouldn't want Mum, my stepfather or Tony to know what I had been up to; he knew I felt ashamed, and that was to be his hold over me.

I went up to my room with Anna and read to her till she fell asleep. I watched her sleep and wondered if my fears for her were real. How could anyone hurt her? She was just a baby.

That night, I couldn't sleep for worrying and decided I would stop Tony from coming to the house. I would keep him away from Fred and the horrible truth about me and my sexual encounters.

The next day, while I sat on the sofa feeding May, I heard Fred and Rose whispering together in the kitchen. When I put May down in her pram, they both came and sat down either side of me. Fred said, 'We've got something to ask you, Caroline. We'd like you to join our "sex circle". You like sex now, so how about it?'

To say I was shocked would be an understatement! Trying not to sound as scared as I felt, I asked, 'What do you mean "sex circle"?'

Fred replied, 'You know – me, you, Rose. You like Rose, don't you?'

I didn't answer that question. Fred went on, 'Yeah, you, me and Rose and a few men friends of ours, you'd enjoy it. You haven't tried a black man yet, have you? You wouldn't want a white man again after being spoilt by a black man, they have bigger dicks, you know, and they know how to fuck. They'd fuck the arse off you. How about it then, are you game for it?'

I couldn't believe that Rose was sitting there letting him speak to me like that. I tried to make light of it and giggled. 'Tell him to behave, Rose.'

But Rose was grinning at me. Nudging me in the side with her elbow, she said, 'Oh, go on, Car, you'll enjoy it, give it a try.'

I could see it wasn't a joke. He was serious and so was Rose. I told them I wasn't into that kind of thing, but they weren't convinced, so I lost my temper and told them I thought I should leave and go back home.

Then Fred got nasty and snarled, 'Do you want me to tell your mum and Tony what you've been up to, 'cause if I do they won't want anything to do with you any more, will they? And that stepfather of yours won't want you back living in his house, will he?'

I started to cry, feeling trapped – and I only had myself to blame for behaving like a little slut. Rose put her arm around me and told me to think about it. Fred got up and left, muttering something about 'fucking lesbians', telling Rose to have it sorted by the time he came back.

Rose had a visitor and went to her room with him, leaving me downstairs feeling sorry for myself. While she was still busy, Roy, one of the two black men who had called to see Rose earlier in the week, came round. He said hello to me and I just burst into tears, much to his embarrassment.

I wondered if he was a member of the sex circle, so when he asked me what was wrong I told him of the obscene thing that Fred and Rose had asked me to do. He seemed genuinely sorry for me and asked me if I would like him to take me home, so I sneaked up to my room, packed what few belongings I had and Roy drove me back home to Cinderford.

When I arrived home, Mum was surprised to see me and asked me why I'd left the Wests. I told her that I hadn't got on with Fred, and left it at that.

6

THE BETRAYAL

ONE MONTH AFTER leaving the Wests, I bumped into them. I had been to see Tony and we spotted them driving past while we were walking around Tewkesbury. I didn't think they had seen us, as they went in the direction of Worcester. Later, I soon realised that they had spotted me, because when Tony left me at my usual spot opposite the Gupshil Manor they pulled up next to me in their old grey Ford Popular again, just like the first time I had met them.

I felt uneasy at seeing them once more, especially after the way I had upped and left without warning. I thought they would have a go at me, but instead Rose got out of the car and said, with a disarming smile, 'Hello, Caroline. How are you? I'm sorry that you left, we have missed you, haven't we, Fred?'

With that, Fred leaned over, looked up at me from inside the car. 'Yeah, and the kids have too,' he added. 'Look, I'm sorry for what I said to you, I was only messing around. Can we give you a lift home?'

My gut feeling told me not to get in the car with them, but it was early December, it was cold and they seemed genuinely sorry about my leaving. I reluctantly gave in and got into the back seat of the car.

No sooner had I sat down than Rose climbed in next to me, saying, 'I'll sit in the back with Caroline, Fred, so we can have a chat.'

As we made our way towards Gloucester, we chatted and I began to relax in their company, but as soon as we got to the Westgate Bridge, which led out of the city and towards my home, things changed. I soon realised that I had made a big mistake.

Fred was looking into the rear-view mirror and staring at me with a hard gaze from his flashing eyes as he asked me, 'Have you had sex with Tony tonight then, Caroline?'

I instantly felt a cold chill run down my spine and I was very afraid of him, but I tried not to show it by saying, 'Oh, don't start all that again!' At the age of seventeen I felt that I'd got over being sexually attacked in the park. It couldn't happen to me twice. I mean, it had never happened to any of my many friends; surely it had been a one-off?

I turned to Rose for support and begged, 'Tell him to leave it, Rose.'

Rose just beamed and said nothing.

Then Fred grinned as he said, 'Have a feel, Rose, see if she's wet.'

With that, Rose grabbed my crutch. In a flash reaction, I

pushed her hand away and stared at her in disbelief! Rose started laughing and began groping at my breasts.

My voice was filled with panic as I shouted at them to leave me alone and to let me out of the car. Crying, I told them, 'I have to get home, let me go, please!'

My fear just seemed to turn them on even more; they were both laughing now. I was fighting with Rose in the cramped space of the back seat, but she was too strong for me. I tugged at her hair and she gave out a yelp, which made Fred join in. His arms were waving and flaying about blindly; he was trying to grab my hair, while still driving. We had just passed the Highnam roundabout when Fred violently pulled the car up on a grass verge.

He turned around in his seat and started lashing out at me, landing a punch on the side of my head. As he was doing this, I could see his tongue jutting out of the side of his lips as if he was concentrating on hitting me on the right spot, the temple. I felt several blows strike me and then I blacked out.

When I came around, my hands were securely tied behind my back with my own scarf. I started to struggle again. Rose was gripping me in a bear hug; her clasp was holding me still while Fred wrapped brown sticky tape around my head and mouth – gagging me.

The driver's door of the car was open; Fred was squatting just inside when he taped me up. My only hope was that someone might drive past and see what he was doing, but no one did. I tried to scream but nothing came out. I pleaded to him with my eyes for him to stop, but he kept going round and round my head with the tape. By now Rose had stopped laughing. She was telling me to be quiet and that I'd be 'all right'. It must have been around 11.30pm when Fred turned the car around and drove back to Cromwell Street. My mind was filled with terror at what lay ahead. I dreaded what they would do to me when they got me back into their lair!

Rose pushed me down into the narrow footwell of the car and even though she was sitting on me, I could tell by the bright street lamps in which direction we were travelling.

The car came to a sudden stop outside their house; Fred went on in to check there was no one about and then came back to give Rose the signal to bring me in.

He told me to be good and added, 'We'll let you go after we've tidied you up a bit.'

I was led into the house and up to the first-floor front bedsit. I'd never been in that particular room before. It was bigger than my old bedroom, which was across the landing from it, next to the bathroom. I could see a table, chairs and a sofa and the floor; next to the window that faced out onto Cromwell Street was a stained double mattress.

I wondered where the children were, and who, if anyone, was looking after them, or if little Anna was left in charge. The house was deadly quiet, with not even the usual sound of music coming from the lodgers' room. I thought to myself that maybe they had left.

Fred sat me on the sofa, told Rose to make a cup of tea and then kneeled down in front of me. He began talking to me softly. 'Look,' he said in a sincere manner, 'Caroline, this has all got out of hand, we didn't want to have to hurt you. If you just calm down, I'll take the tape off, but you have to promise to keep quiet.'

I nodded that I would do as he asked, and with that he took a knife and started to cut the tape away from the side of my head. I winced as I felt a burning sensation, and he stopped, 'Oh shit! I'm sorry, I've cut you, it's a bloody double-bladed knife!'

Rose came in with three cups of tea. Fred went out of the room and came back with a pair of scissors and continued to cut the tape from me. Rose was making little soothing noises: 'There, there, don't cry, you'll be all right,' trying her best to keep me calm.

The tape had stuck to my hair and it was hurting as Fred pulled it away. He was being very gentle and kept apologising to me. It was hard to believe that this was the same man who, twenty minutes earlier, had been thumping me around the head and snarling abuse at me. Once the tape was off, Fred picked up his cup of tea, pulled a chair up and sat in front of me, while Rose sat next to me on the sofa.

I couldn't grasp what was going on – one minute they had been attacking me, the next they were being nice to me and saying sorry. They were chatting to me as if nothing was unusual about the situation.

'Guess what?' Fred said 'Rose has got a bun in the oven. She's three months gone now; we're hoping for a boy this time. Wouldn't you like to come back here to live? Rose really needs you now.'

Rose snuggled up next to me and smiled as she said, 'Go on, Car, say you'll come back. I've missed you and the kids have. It will be better this time, promise.'

I put on a brave face and smiled, too scared to say anything in case I broke into tears and annoyed them. They untied my hands so I could drink my tea, and they gave me a cigarette, which helped to calm me down. I thought I would be safe as long as I played along with them. I didn't try to shout for help, as there was no one there who could help me.

Even if Ben was there, he would either have been asleep or stoned out of his head like a zombie – so would his friends. And besides, I didn't know if they were part of the West sex circle or not. At that moment, I felt I was reasonably safe, as they had stopped attacking me and seemed to have come to their senses. Once again I was wrong.

Rose finished her tea off by gulping the remains down and then put her arm around my shoulder and kissed me full on the mouth. I moved away from her and shut my lips up tight. My rejection only made things worse and she became angry.

Pushing her away, I shouted at her, 'Fuck off, fucking leave me alone!'

With that, Fred held me down and pressed my head, face first, into the sofa, telling Rose to 'get the cotton wool'. I could hear Rose scuttle off. She returned in a flash with the cotton wool and, as Fred lifted my head up, she rammed a big wad of it into my mouth. I was retching on it, then they got what looked like a strip of torn-up white sheeting and tied it around my head to keep the cotton wool in place. As they worked on silencing me, they were cursing and calling me names.

They stood me up and started to undress me, still cursing me: 'Keep fucking quiet, you stupid fucking bitch!'

Fred raised his clenched fist to me and said, 'Do you want some more of this, bitch?'

In response, I vigorously shook my head and started crying again.

'Just do as you're fucking told and you'll be all right,' he screamed at me, as he pulled my arms behind my back and bound my wrists together with some orange-coloured rope.

I realised by now that there was no way I could take both of them on and get out of the house safely, so I resigned myself to the fact that, if I wanted to get out of there in one piece, I would have to go along with whatever it was they were going to do to me.

Fred led me over to the stained mattress and told me to lie down. I could see Rose staring at me as she got undressed. I curled up into the foetal position, trying to hide as much of my naked body as I could.

As she came towards me I felt sick. I rolled over, half on my front, burying my face in the pillow, not wanting to see her flabby nakedness.

As she lay next to me, I had a sudden urge to kick out at her, but I knew better than to antagonise her again. I lay there like a wretch and tried to think about something else. My mum's face flashed into my head and I thought what it would be like for her if I never made it home again. I knew it would kill her.

Rose rolled me over on to my back. My arms were under the weight of my body and my shoulder blades hurt like crazy. Her hands were running all over my body. I turned away from her again, a more than deliberate move on my part to avoid her repulsive touch.

Fred growled at me, 'Keep fucking still, you bitch! Rose isn't going to hurt you!'

Her clammy hands were continuously pawing at me and her fingers entered into every crevice of my body. When she pinched my nipples hard with her finger ends, I gave out a muffled shriek. I felt her searching fingers go deeper in between my legs. I thought I was going to vomit and choke to death on it. I wriggled away from her again and she pulled me back to her again.

'What's wrong with you, haven't you ever had a woman before? Relax and enjoy,' she purred, over and over again. She was like a Svengali trying to hypnotise me into a trance-like state. 'Relax and enjoy, relax and enjoy.'

Rose moved down the mattress and wrenched my legs apart in a violent manner. Automatically, I closed them. No one had ever been that close to my genitals before; no boyfriend had ever seen me naked. I was very self-conscious and shy of my private area being exposed. I had always kept myself covered up or made love in the dark. My legs were now closed up tight like a vice; I had no control over them at all. I knew this would make my two attackers angry, but I couldn't help it.

Rose looked up at Fred, who was stood at the end of the mattress watching what was going on, at the same time rubbing his erect penis through his jeans.

He said, 'You wanna hand there, Rosie?'

He got down on his knees. They each took one of my legs and prised them apart as if pulling a wishbone between them. His grip around my ankle, tighter than hers, was giving me an unremitting pain. I soon forgot about this when I felt Rose's hot, intense breath between my legs as she took a good look.

Fred saw her looking and said, 'What do ya think then,

Rose?' as if she had just opened a gift he'd given her, or finished a job he was proud of.

'Why don't you come and have a look for yourself,' she said, grinning at him.

Fred picked up another strip of the white cloth. He lifted my head up and tied it around my head, covering my eyes.

At first, I was almost grateful, that I couldn't see the sight of them inspecting my most intimate parts. Strangely enough, I had it in my head that if I couldn't see them, then they couldn't see me with my legs splayed apart like a spring chicken.

I felt Fred climb on to the mattress next to me. The suddenness of his rough, thick fingers, like sandpaper on my skin, made me jump and squirm in horror, closing my legs automatically. The comfort I had at first gained from the blindfold was now gone.

My legs were yanked apart once more. Rose and Fred's bodies were both squeezed between them. I now felt two hands on me – one was small and soft and the other one was big and rough. The soft hand was stroking me; the big rough hand was pulling and prodding at me.

Two lots of fingers were forced inside my most intimate part, making me squeal out in agony as the faceless fingers searched and probed with an unrelenting fervour. During this probing part of their molestation, all the while the two of them were discussing my genitals as if they were experts on the subject.

'She's big inside, ain't she, Rose?'

'Yeah, and she hasn't even had any kids yet,' Rose replied.

'Her lips are too fat,' Fred said matter-of-factly, referring to my vulva.

'They cover her clit, no wonder she doesn't enjoy sex!'

They were examining me like a couple of seasoned gynaecologists, and as that thought went through my mind, I began to panic again as I remembered Fred's bragging about abortions he had performed. My fear intensified as he referred to his observations and added, 'I can put that right for her.'

His words sent a chill down my spine; I dreaded what he had in mind. I started to retch again as I suddenly realised he was going to operate on me while I was awake!

At that moment I would rather have died than feel myself being mutilated. I struggled, thrashing and twisting my head from side to side trying to get the blindfold off so I could plead with him, with my eyes, not to do it.

The cotton wool had made my mouth dry and I couldn't manage to get a sound to come out even though I was trying to call his name. Right then I would have promised him the world and done anything he wanted, willingly and with a smile on my face, just as long as he did not operate.

I was literally in a blind terror as to what surgical skills he would next reveal. Up until that point I was convinced I would be all right if I just let them get on with it. I'd been abused in the past and I'd got over it, but the thought of being cut and having parts of my vagina sliced off was too much for me to cope with.

I could feel Fred stand up. I thought, this is it, he's going to fetch his scalpel.

Rose loosened her grip on my leg; I turned over on my tummy and rubbed my face into the pillow. As the tears of fear soaked into the white cotton blindfold, it rolled up slightly and I could see. My arms had gone numb from being under my weight all the time. I began to get some feeling back and just then I was pulled roughly over onto my back again. Fred had taken his belt off and stood there looking down on me, observing me.

With a sadistic pleasure in his voice, he roared 'This is for your own good, you'll enjoy sex much more after this.'

He then dragged me to the edge of the mattress as I writhed trying to get away from what unknown horror I faced.

Then he ordered Rose, 'Hold her legs open, Rose.' She did as he said.

Then he folded his leather belt in half, grasped it in his hand, raised it high above his head and bought it down in a hard frenzy upon my vagina. The blow sent a shockwave of pain through me and sent my body into a spasm. This was the first blow of what was to be a whipping frenzy. He struck me about six times; it stung and pulsated like hell. The buckle part of the belt, glistening in the light, was hitting its target with non-stop accuracy. Between each welt the evil came through Fred's flashing eyes. I was certain that I must be badly cut. I sobbed as they let me close my legs; my beaten flesh was burning hot and throbbing with pain.

Rose went to the bathroom and returned with some cold water in a bowl. Now she was transformed from the sadistic, demonic, sex-crazed beast into the more recognisable form of the soft-speaking Gloucestershire housewife.

She told me to turn over, saying she wanted to bathe me, to clean me up and cool me down. She rinsed me down with some cotton wool. The cool water helped relieve some of the stinging pain, but it didn't take all the pain away caused by the whipping.

Fred left the room and soon returned with three more cups of tea. Once again, they were being nice to me.

'If you promise to be good,' Fred said, soothingly, 'I'll take the gag off so you can have a drink.'

I nodded in agreement, and he untied the gag and pulled the damp cotton wool out of my mouth. My mouth and throat were so dry that when I tried to speak, I was hardly able to mutter a coherent word; my voice was rasping.

I begged, 'Can you untie my hands, please, my arms are hurting. I promise, I'll not try anything. Please?'

He took the blindfold off me without being asked, then he unfastened my hands. There were rope burns round my wrists where he had replaced my scarf with the rope.

As I held the cup of tea and brought it to my lips, my hands shook in an uncontrollable action. I sipped the tea as best I could, checking the heat. Then, to relieve my thirst, filled my mouth with it and gargled before swallowing. Fred gave me a cigarette and went on about how the beating with the belt would flatten out my vaginal lips, exposing my clitoris, and how it would improve my sensitivity during sex.

'You'll thank me for it one day,' he exalted, whilst smiling and winking at me.

That remark put a seed of optimism in my mind. I took it to mean that I would live to see another day.

I tried to reassure them that they could trust me not to say anything if they let me go. I said I would be too embarrassed to tell anyone what had gone on. I knew they hadn't finished with me, however, when Fred told me, 'Just do as you're told and you'll be all right,' as he retied my hands behind my back again.

I pleaded with him not to use the gag again. 'I won't call for help, please!'

'You shout and we'll fucking kill ya, bitch,' Fred hissed.

He ordered me to lie down on the mattress, Rose lay beside me and kissed me full on the mouth, I didn't respond; I couldn't. As much as my life may have depended on it, I couldn't bring myself to kiss her back. All I could do was lie there like a tailor's dummy and allow her to do what she wanted to do to me, however much it repulsed me. All I could think about was going home, and how late it was. I wondered if my mum was still sat up reading in bed and wondering where I was. Then I thought, she'll think I'm staying at Tony's 'cause I hadn't got a lift. I had done that once before.

As Rose once again squeezed my nipples, making me squirm away from her, thoughts of home vanished. Fred, who was stood watching, grunted at me to keep still. Not wanting to be gagged again, I lay frozen.

My legs were splayed apart. Rose, in an act that turned my stomach, went down on me and started licking between my legs. I had never experienced oral sex before; I felt it was far too intimate an act, one that I was too shy to try. I would have to completely trust my lover first before I would open myself up to that much sensitivity. There I was, lying vulnerably open, without any say in the matter. This was an act that had far surpassed the boundaries of anything I had ever experienced. To have my first experience of oral sex forced upon me by a woman was a sickening and shaming experience. I felt I was going to throw up there and then. I took deep breaths to stop me panicking.

The sounds of his wife's sick and perverted pleasure turned Fred on. His manhood was aroused again and he stood there openly masturbating. It was disgusting.

They were talking dirty to each other, 'You're enjoying that, aren't you ... you dirty cow.'

'Yeah, you can join in now if you want,' Rose said, flirting with her husband.

Fred took his jeans off and had sex with Rose from behind, doggy style, while she kept her attention on me. This was like something out of a top-shelf porn magazine, the kind I had seen in Alf's private box when I was snooping one day. The images in the magazine had shocked and yet titillated me at the same time. Being a part of this threesome was not titillating though; it was simply degrading.

I turned away again, sickened at the sight of seeing the two of them, like animals, grunting, groaning and thrashing together in their fornication. I suppose this went on for ten minutes, but to me it seemed like hours.

When they had both finished, I could smell the semen that was running down Rose's legs; she went to the bathroom to wipe herself down. Then it was time for another cup of tea and a cigarette. This time they both left the room, leaving me trussed up naked to a chair; the dirty gag was back in place. 'It's just till we get back,' Rose assured me.

I felt that if I could put up with all they had done, I could hold out till morning. They were gone for about twenty minutes. When they came back, they untied me and took the gag off. I sat there exhausted and shocked by the events of the night. I wanted to sleep; I needed to sleep. I yawned, and they yawned too.

'We think you should stay here a few days, Car, till we know we can trust you. If you behave, you can stay in this room, if not … then you'll be kept in the cellar,' said Fred.

The alarming thought of being kept in the cellar was too much for me to bear. I had never been in it, but I knew it would be dark, dank and creepy, and I was petrified of cellars. The eerie creations within my imagination had made me scared stiff. I pictured all sorts of monsters, ghosts and fiends lying in wait in the darkness down below. My fear grew from a callous act previously carried out by my brothers: they had locked me in the cupboard under the stairs at home. I was terrified, kicking at the door and screaming for them to let me out. Visions of reliving this nightmare caught me off guard and sent a shudder of fear running through my whole body. Because of this, I tried all the more to convince them that they could trust me, and told them that my mum would call the police if she didn't hear from me soon.

They started on again about their sex circle and how they thought I would soon get to enjoy it. I felt all my hopes of going home were now dashed. They had tricked me into thinking I could go home so that I would be easier to handle.

Fred said he had to get some sleep because he had work later that morning. They tied my arms up, put me under the sheets and then climbed in next to me. I pretended to go to sleep. I lay there wondering how I could escape from the situation. Then I remembered that the milkman called around early in Cromwell Street. Yes, that was it, if only I could get the milkman's attention, I might at least have an eyewitness to my being there.

When I was sure Fred and Rose were both asleep, I managed

to extricate myself from between them and get myself up off the mattress and over to the window. To have made it to the door I would have had to climb over them, and then, as far as I knew, the door was locked.

I made it to the window without waking either one of them, slipped quietly through the gap in the curtain and stood there naked. I pressed my face hard against the icy-cold glass and strained to look up and down the road, past the condensation that was quickly forming caused by my hot, steamy breath.

As I wiped the condensation, the glass made a squeaking noise and I froze with fear. I could hear my heart pounding in my chest as I listened to see if the noise had disturbed my captors. I had to see if anyone was up and about, but my hot, panting breath engulfed the glass even more – my own living breath had become my enemy! I turned my back to the window and tried to lift the sash frame with my tied hands, but my 5ft 2in frame wasn't tall enough to reach it.

Defeated and distraught, I crept back on to the mattress, lay down and waited for my chance to break out. I decided on my escape plan, which I played through my head. I would make a run for it when they let me out of the room to take me to the cellar. I would kick my way out!

I felt ashamed of myself for being weak and simply lying there while they did all of those vile, disgusting, degrading things to me. I was angry that I had trusted them to release me; they had fooled me into a false sense of security. They had used me, abused me and betrayed me.

Rose had betrayed me most, because she was a friend; it was because of her that I had given them a second chance and got into their car. I could not have prophesied what she was planning to do to me. Women are supposed to be nurturers, emotional people, protective and supportive of each other. They did not sexually abuse. Yet she had and I hated her for it.

The thought of being locked up in the cellar had jolted me to my senses; I no longer believed I would be released. I had to fight for my life.

I realised it would be easier to escape when Anna and the lodgers were awake. Even if I didn't get out of the house, someone would see me, and when Mum sent the police searching for me, which she would surely do, she would send them to Tony's. And Tony would remember we had seen the Wests driving through Tewkesbury; he would point the finger at my weird ex-employers. But how long would all that take?

I was trying to stay awake, but must have dropped off to sleep for a short time. Suddenly, I was startled by the sound of a bell, a doorbell. I woke up not knowing where I was, and then I recalled what had happened to me, thinking initially that it must have been a nightmare of sorts. But I couldn't move my hands – they were bound tight – and this was real. I collected my thoughts.

I lay there, eyes closed, pretending to be asleep. Fred jumped up and pulled his jeans on. He woke Rose and whispered to her, 'Keep her quiet, there's someone at the door.'

Then I heard Fred coming back up the stairs, talking to another man. I didn't recognise the voice, but it was definitely not a Jamaican accent. I still didn't know if the man was one of their sex circle.

Fred came back into the room, leaving the man outside the door. That was when I decided that this man was not part of the

Wests' plans for my involvement in the sex circle. This was my chance; I took a deep breath and shouted out, 'Help me! Get …' Rose pressed a pillow over my face and put her upper body weight on it, smothering me. At first, I struggled then I played dead, hoping she would lift the pillow.

My thoughts of how I would die came back to haunt me. I thought, this is it: I'm going to die, the air in my lungs will ebb away! Then, suddenly, the pillow was lifted. I gasped! Gulping for air, I swallowed a mouthful. Slowly, as the dizziness subsided, I opened my eyes. What greeted me wasn't a pretty sight… I saw Fred's repulsive face looking down on me. In the cold light of day, his stark features made him look uglier than ever, his face contorted into a gargoylian look of anger, He grabbed me by the throat and lifted me up off the mattress.

'You fucking stupid little bitch,' Fred hissed. 'You've had it now!'

Rose grabbed my hair and pulled me to towards her while cursing me. They were both talking at the same time, calling me names. I thought they were going to kill me there and then, which would have been a relief at the time. To my horror, they spoke words to me that I will never forget: 'We are going to keep you in the cellar and let our black friends use you and when they have finished with you, we will kill you and bury you under the paving stones of Gloucester. There are hundreds of girls there, the police haven't found them and they won't find you!'

Still snarling at me, the Wests brutally forced a fresh wad of cotton wool into my mouth and tied it secure with the white material. I lay there on my side on the mattress in stunned silence as they hurriedly half-dressed themselves.

All I could think of was how my poor mum would cope if I didn't make it home. A vision of my mum's crying face kept flashing through my mind. I began to cry, not for me, but for her. How could I have put her through all that misery? I started on a journey of self-deprecation. I had always been a cause for anxiety to her. If I hadn't been born she would have been spared a lot of heartache, but I had been born and she had loved me, unconditionally.

I had been through the most horrific ordeal; I had given the Wests the benefit of the doubt and they had conned me. I imagined myself tied up in the cellar, and all the men who had been regular visitors to the house grabbing, prodding, pushing and squeezing at me. It crossed my mind that they could have some poor girl, just like me, tied up down in the cellar already, and that I was to join her! Yes, that was it! This was their sex circle! Is that why the men came round when I was living there? Was this happening below my very feet as I sat watching TV? I couldn't stop the dreadful thoughts that came flooding into my mind, intensifying my fear.

The reverberation of footsteps on the stairs interrupted my thoughts. Fred went out on to the landing. I could hear Anna's voice; the baby needed feeding. I did consider trying to make a noise, but I knew it could put Anna in danger too, so I waited to see what was going to happen next.

I heard Rose order Anna back to the bedroom, and then they were whispering again. Fred returned to the room on his own, shutting the door behind him. Locking it. He stood looking at me intently. He walked towards me, kneeled down and caressed my breasts, saying, 'It's OK. I'm not going to hurt you.' Then his calloused hand went down and he stuck it between my legs. I moved away but he gently pulled me on to my back.

He seemed mesmerised, in a trance-like state, as he slowly moved his hands over my body. After a few minutes he took his hand away, but not his eyes. Then there was a second of awestruck hesitation as he glanced over his shoulder at the locked door.

As he took his jeans off, I shook my head and started to cry. 'Don't cry,' he cooed but I couldn't help it. He positioned himself on me, entering me, stroking my hair and whispering, 'It's OK. It's OK.'

After a minute or two, he stopped and withdrew himself from me. He didn't go all the way, he never ejaculated. It was like he just had to have a dabble, a taster of me to see what I was like.

I began to sob, really sob. I wasn't sobbing because he had raped me, but because now even he had gone too far, and because of his actions he would definitely have to kill me. The consequences of his behaviour didn't stir him because he knew he could get away with it.

He pulled his jeans back on and sat down next to me, patting my thigh. 'I'm sorry, Car, I shouldn't have done that.' His voice faltered and wavered as he spoke. I turned and looked at him and was shocked to see that he was crying. Unfeigned tears filled his eyes. He looked a pathetic sight. I felt embarrassed by his unexpected outburst. The last time I had seen a grown man cry had been in a similar situation. The old man that had indecently assaulted me in Gloucester Park when I was thirteen years old had cried uncontrollably when he was caught. I had felt sorry for him, and now I was beginning to feel sorry for a pitiable

Fred, yet they had both hurt me and had cared nothing for my feelings. I was so confused; I just buried my head in the mattress and sobbed.

Then came the next shock, 'You mustn't tell Rose what I did, Car,' he said in a pitiful voice as he looked me in the eye. 'She'll be really pissed off with both of us! You see, you were here solely for Rose's pleasure, not mine. When Rose is pregnant, she gets these lesbian urges and she has to have a woman, and she wanted you. She'll kill both of us if she finds out!'

He looked nervously at the door then back to me and quickly said, 'If you don't tell her and promise me you'll come back here to live, I'll let you go.' I didn't know if this was another one of his tricks but I had no choice, I had to believe him. He was giving me a chance and I had to take it.

I nodded, yes. 'You know, if you do tell anyone or you don't come back, my black friends will come looking for you,' he whispered to me.

I frantically nodded my head.

'OK, I'll go and tell Rose, she'll be so pleased,' he said in a more normal tone of voice.

He stood up, went to the door and then, having second thoughts, he came back and said, 'I told Rose I was going to tie you to the chair, so I'll have to. Just now she's looking after the kids. I'll go and tell her that you want to come back here to live, OK?'

He seemed almost jovial as he left the room and, although I was left naked, gagged and bound to the chair, I felt optimistic because, somehow, I believed he would keep his word. As the feeling of relief overwhelmed me, tears streamed down my face.

Some ten minutes later, Rose came into the room with Fred in tow right behind her. He must have been convincing when he told Rose that I wanted to come back and live with them because Rose rushed over to me, smiling all over her face, and she hugged me.

Fred was watching my face closely. I guess he was worried I might change my mind and spill the beans, but I wasn't that stupid. Rose ran me a bath and helped me to wash my hair, which was still sticky from the gum on the tape that they had first gagged me with. With only a towel wrapped around me, I sat there allowing Fred to brush the remnants of the gum out, but my hair was too knotty, so I got back in the bath and lay down trying to soak the gum out of my hair, combing it through a few strands at a time.

It was better than before, but some hair was coiled up where it had been heaved at by the tape, so Fred took the scissors and snipped at it here and there. By the time he had finished it looked tidy.

I noticed some bruising around one of my cheeks. I had rope burns around my wrists, my torso, under one of my breasts and around my back from where I had been tied to the chair, but otherwise I looked pretty normal again.

An hour after being raped and thinking I was going to die, I was dressed and sitting on the sofa drinking tea and smoking a cigarette, with Rose sat next to me, stroking my hair and chatting to me as if nothing untoward had ever happened.

All my life I had covered up my true emotions to protect others and myself, and now all that acting was about to pay off. I played the part of the caring nanny again as Fred brought the children into the room.

'Look who's come to see us,' he proclaimed to the children.

Anna-Marie, who was already dressed ready for school, looked shyly at me.

I said, 'Hello, Anna, do I get a hug?'

She walked over to me with a little smile on her face. I pulled her towards me and hugged her, kissed her on the cheek and ruffled her short, boyish hair.

'Are you back for good?' she asked, almost whispering.

I felt terrible lying to her, as I felt she was relieved that I might be around to protect her. 'Yes, Anna. I'm coming back; can I have my old room back? Do you mind if we share again?'

She seemed to cheer up and went off to school happy in the knowledge that I would be there when she got back. I hated having to lie to her, but I needed to convince Fred and Rose that I would be moving back in that evening.

Heather came toddling over to me; I picked her up and gave her a cuddle and she sat on my lap while she finished her bottle of tea.

Meanwhile, Fred had passed baby May to Rose, who was getting her dressed. Fred asked if I would help Rose out with the kids and housework while he dropped Anna-Marie at school; then he would drop me, Rose and the kids off at the launderette. I did as he said and, while Rose fed the girls, I tidied up and vacuumed the room. Then I sat down next to Rose on the sofa and waited for Fred to come back.

The first sign of anyone besides the West family being in the house caused me to jump, as I heard a knock on the door. Ben peeped his head around the door. He seemed surprised to see me. 'All right, Caroline?' I felt relief and embarrassment all at once. Relief that he was now a witness to me being there, and embarrassment at the memory of the night his roommate kicked me out.

'Yeah, I'm all right,' I answered. Then I looked at Rose, who was looking flustered. I knew what she was thinking. She was afraid that I would blurt everything out to Ben. But I had no intentions of doing that. If he had been in the house and had heard anything, he hadn't made any attempt to find out what was going on, and I still didn't know who was in and who was out of the Wests' sex circle.

'Can I use the Hoover, Rose?' Ben asked, looking as embarrassed as I felt. After picking up the Hoover, he left the room.

I figured he was not one of the sex circle, for two reasons: firstly because he looked as if he had walked in on something he shouldn't have, and secondly because of Rose's reaction. She looked guilty and frightened. If he were one of her cronies, she would have been more relaxed.

At about 9.30am, Fred came back and the three of us sat and drank another cup of tea while they went over again how I was not to tell anybody about what had gone on, and how Fred had friends that would come after me if I went to the police. I made my promises, anything that I thought would convince them that it was safe to let me go.

We all got into the car and drove to the launderette on Eastgate Street. It was such a relief to get out of the house that I nearly cried, but managed to keep the tears at bay.

Fred carried the bags in for us, we carried the girls in, and Fred gave me a final warning. 'I'll see you later then.'

I nodded and said, 'Yeah, OK.'

I held baby May while Rose sorted her washing into two machines, then she sat down next to me, looking very nervous. She wasn't as confident now that Fred was out of the picture and I was out of her domain at the house. I waited ten minutes, gave May to Rose to hold, told her I had to go for some cigarettes and left before she could argue with me.

I walked out of the launderette and just kept on walking, down to the cross, down Westgate Street, past the turnoff to Bearlands Police Station and over Westgate Bridge. I didn't look around, I didn't look back, just straight forward, all my thoughts focused on getting home.

I would have walked all the way home but for a friend's brother who stopped and offered me a lift. When I first heard his Mini pulling up beside me, I ignored it. For a minute, I thought Rose had managed to phone Fred at the Permlais factory where he worked. I kept walking, thinking he wouldn't dare try to abduct me in broad daylight. It wasn't until I heard Colin Taylor's voice that I stopped and turned. 'Caroline, Caroline! Do you want a lift?'

I got in the car, lay back and relaxed. I gave out a long sigh of relief. Knowing I was safe at last, I lay my head back against the headrest and closed my eyes.

'Thanks, Colin, thanks a lot. You're my saviour.' Which I was sure he was. I wasn't in the mood for pleasantries, so I went on, 'I'm so tired, I didn't get any sleep last night.'

He asked, 'What you been doing in Gloucester then?'

I told him I had stayed at my boyfriend's the night before night and had no money for the bus fare home.

'Oh, that's why you didn't get any sleep,' he said with a knowing grin.

I made my tiredness an excuse to rest my eyes and didn't speak to Colin again until he dropped me off in Cinderford High Street, where I thanked him once more and said, 'See ya!'

As I walked the five minutes to Northwood Close, I preoccupied myself with the problem of how to get into my house and up to my bed without Mum questioning me. I couldn't have coped if she had questioned me about where I had spent the night. I wasn't very good at lying to Mum; she could usually recognise by my blushing when I had lied or been up to no good.

Instead of going straight home, I went to visit my mate, Doreen, who lived at the end of our road. It was Doreen that I had lived with in Portsmouth. We had shared many secrets, so it was Doreen I turned to. I confided in Doreen and told her that the Wests had abducted me and that they had both carried out depraved sexual acts on me. I couldn't give her all the gory details. I didn't trust her that much.

Doreen advised me that I should tell the police, but that was the last thing I wanted to do. I didn't want to talk about it ever again. After the last sexual assault against me in Gloucester Park, I wasn't keen on reliving being made to look the tease.

All I wanted was to get into my own bed, go to sleep and wake up to find that it had all been a bad dream.

7

THE ACCUSED

I LAY CURLED up in my bed with my head under the blankets and tried to sleep. But the sleep I longed for didn't come. Instead, in my head, I was going over and over the events of the previous night.

Why did I get in the car? If only I had run away and gone to Jock and Hilda's who Tony was staying with, none of it would have happened. Why didn't I do that? I didn't want to be a nuisance, that's why. I didn't like imposing on people. I was sure they would have felt obliged to take me home and I was sure Tony would have been annoyed with me for putting them in that position.

I felt Tony had been pretty cool towards me recently – or maybe I was just feeling paranoid with guilt about the other men I had slept with while I was supposed to be his girlfriend. I hated myself for what I had done to Tony. I hated myself for getting in that car when my inner voice was telling me not to. I had never listened to my inner voice. It was as if I had been dared to defy it. I had to push my luck, always knowing that I'd come a cropper.

It was like being on a mission of suicide. Only this time, I had come very close to succeeding. I felt it was my own fault and that I deserved what I had got. And later that day, and over the following days, I was to find that others felt I had asked for it too.

I kept going over and over what had happened to me. Why was I such a coward? Why didn't I shout for help? I argued with myself that even if I had screamed out, who would have bothered to investigate the noise?

I came to the conclusion that no one would have helped or got involved. And when I did shout, it had nearly cost me my life after Rose smothered me with the pillow. I couldn't have run away as Rose and Fred led me into their house because I was trussed up and gagged like a Christmas turkey. I simply should not have got into their car in the first place. I should have run, run for my life.

Later that day, Mum came up into my bedroom, sat on my bed and offered me a cup of tea. I kept my face under the blankets and snapped, 'I don't want anything to drink, just leave me alone. I'm tired. Please go away!'

Then the tears came. Mum asked, 'Whatever is the matter with you, Caroline?'

Then she asked the question she always asked when I was upset: 'Have you and Tony fell out or something?'

I didn't answer. I didn't want to lie to Mum, but I didn't want to tell her the truth either. Later that day, Mum went to see

Doreen to ask her what was wrong and Doreen told her as much as she knew.

Mum came straight back home to confront me with it. She asked, 'Tell me what they did to you. Are you hurt?'

I began to cry, and then Mum began to cry too. I hated hearing her cry and tried to console her, saying nothing had happened. 'I want to help you, Caroline,' she said to me, 'Don't lie!'

She pulled the blankets back off my face and reeled back in horror when she saw my swollen eyes. She gasped, 'We have to call the police, Caroline, tell me what have they done to you!'

'I don't want to talk about it, Mum. I just want to forget about it. Please, leave me alone,' I replied.

I heard Alf come in. 'Don't tell him, Mum,' I pleaded, to no avail. Before I could finish the sentence, she was charging down the stairs. I buried my head under the blankets again and cried. I knew what Alf's reaction would be, and I was right. I could hear their raised voices. Mum was standing up to Alf.

I could hear Alf telling Mum, 'I don't want the police up here, she'll get over it.'

Mum was having none of it. Later, when Alf went out to the pub, she phoned the police and soon afterwards a large policewoman in her forties came lumbering into the bedroom and started to speak to me while Mum watched. I cowered under the blanket. The policewoman pulled the blanket off me and said she needed to see my injuries.

She looked at my face and asked, 'Have you had a fight with your boyfriend?'

'No,' I replied.

She asked me, in a regimented way, 'Would you like to tell me where you were all night and what has happened to you? Your mother says you were attacked by your former employers, is that right?' I didn't want to answer her. I wished Mum had just left me alone. Alf obviously thought I was just making it up for attention, or that I had it coming to me due to the way I behaved.

The policewoman was annoyed with me; I could tell from her tone of voice. She asked me if I would like my mum to leave the room and I nodded. I didn't want Mum to know what I had been through, as it would have given her nightmares. Reluctantly, Mum left the policewoman and me alone.

'Have you any other injuries?' The policewoman asked.

I began to cry as I pulled back my sleeves and showed her the rope burns around my wrists. Then I pulled my top up and showed her my back; a rope burn went around my back where my bra would have been.

I didn't dare show her my genital area, even though there were some red marks over it. I didn't want anyone to look at or touch that area. I was still sore and it was too much of an intimate a place to show this big, hard-faced policewoman.

'Right, let's get some details down,' she said, her voice suddenly softening.

I gave her some of the details, which she wrote down in her notebook. It was 10.00pm when she had first shown up. An hour later she left, taking away the clothes that I had been wearing the night before and telling me that someone would be out to see me in the morning. I noticed the button had come off my trousers sometime during the night; maybe they would find it at the Wests' house.

For hours after that I couldn't get any sleep. I wondered if the police would go straight around to arrest the Wests that night and what lies they would tell the police about me. I was sure they would try to deny it all. My hope was that Ben, the lodger, had seen me and that if they questioned him he would tell them I was there. Then I worried even more about what they would say about me to get away with what they had done. I also kept going over and over what they had threatened me with.

Had they really done it to other girls?

Had they kept a girl in the cellar while I lived there?

Had they really buried hundreds of girls under the paving stones of Gloucester?

By the time I dropped into a restless slumber it was daylight.

Alf was furious with Mum for calling the police. I heard them arguing again. Alf stormed out of the house early.

My sister, Sue, woke me with a cup of tea before leaving for school and asked, 'What's happened? Why are the police taking you away, have you been fighting?'

I told her that the Wests had attacked me, but I didn't want to talk about it. Sue was only twelve years old, but very feisty.

'I'll fucking kill the bastards,' she said as she scanned my face and hair before she left the room.

Before I went downstairs, I waited for everyone to leave for work and school. I was glad Alf had gone; he obviously thought I had asked for it. I knew Phillip would be thinking the same; after all, his little sister had always been an embarrassment to him.

While we were waiting for the police to come, a local man from the estate came with a new washing machine for Mum.

He took one look at me and said, 'What on earth have you been up to?' I ran out of the room on the edge of tears and left Mum to explain.

When the police arrived, they had a photographer with them. I was taken into the lounge and had my injuries photographed. Still I didn't mention the injury marks caused by the belt buckle on my genital area.

I gave a statement to DC Jones; it was one of the hardest things I had ever done. I didn't want to talk about it; I just wanted to forget about it. The more questions they asked, the more I wished Mum had never called the police. Talking about it kept it real, when all I wanted to do was forget it, to let it become a bad dream.

Hours later, Mum and I were taken to the police surgeon at the end of Worcester Street, in Gloucester. Mum had insisted on being with me. I wished she hadn't, it just made it harder for me. I still didn't tell them anything about my genital injuries. I couldn't have beared to be touched or examined by anyone, either male or female.

We were taken back to Bearlands Police Station, where I was led into a room full of policemen and women. I was asked to pull up my jumper and show them my injuries. I felt so embarrassed and self-conscious. I wished the floor would open and swallow me up. I was so glad I had kept my other injuries from them or I would have had to take my pants off too and they would all have seen my 'abnormal' vagina. I cringed as the thought went through my mind and I began to cry.

When we were walking through the car park back to the police car, I walked ahead of Mum with DC Jones. I felt he knew I was hiding something, then he quietly asked me if there had been any penetration.

'What do you mean?' I asked him.

He looked me in the eye and said, 'Did Fred have intercourse with you, did he put his penis inside you?'

I looked behind me to make sure Mum wasn't close enough to hear us and then, in almost a whisper, I said, 'Yes, but it didn't last long.'

DC Jones stopped in his tracks and with a look of confusion on his face said, 'But you didn't mention it before, it isn't in your statement. How come?'

I kept walking for fear of Mum listening and he followed.

'I'm sorry but I had forgotten about it,' I said.

He looked astonished as he said, 'How could you forget something like that?'

'I told you, it didn't last long, only a minute or so, and besides, he said he was sorry,' I replied with a defensive tone to my voice.

DC Jones shook his head in disbelief and asked me, 'Did he ejaculate inside you, did he come?'

'No, he didn't, he only did it for a minute. He was scared Rose would walk in and catch him,' I replied.

Still shaking his head in disbelief, he called to the other officer over and whispered to him. Mum had caught up with me by then and asked me what was going on. I told her I had forgotten something, but didn't explain what it was.

DC Jones came back to me and said, 'We will have to do another statement. You should have told us.'

I felt he was angry with me and I started to fill up. We drove home in silence, my head hanging down in shame. I could feel my mum's eyes on me, but she didn't ask me anything else while we were in the car.

When we were alone at home, I told Mum I had been raped, and she started to cry. I tried to make her understand that it was all over in a minute and that he hadn't hurt me. But I guess it didn't help her much.

I had forgotten the fact that I had been raped, something no one would understand. How could anyone forget something as traumatic as being raped? The next day, I went to Cinderford Police Station to make another statement. I tried to explain to the police that I was so shocked and repulsed by everything else that had happened to me during the time I was with the Wests that the intercourse part was the only 'normal' thing that had taken place. I'd had sex before and this time it didn't last very long. He was very gentle with me and was making soothing sounds while he did it. It was not aggressive and, although I was sore, it still didn't hurt as much as any of the other things they had done to me.

I was not used to being kidnapped and sexually assaulted or kissed by a woman. I was not used to being punched unconscious, being tied up and gagged. I was not used to having a woman carry out vile sexual acts on me or having two people mess with me down below. I was not used to being beaten with a belt on my vaginal area. I was not used to being smothered and being in fear for my life. All these things had been alien to me. All these things had put the fear of death into me.

The rape, an act of sexual intercourse, was, compared to the rest of my ordeal, the only thing I was used to – the norm. The more I thought about it, it was the rape that had shown me that

Fred did have a little bit of compassion in him. Seeing him cry had made me feel pity for him, just as I had felt sorry for the old man that had sexually assaulted me when I was thirteen years old. Fred's fear of Rose finding out that he had raped me had, in my mind, saved my life.

The police still found this earlier omission in my statement hard to understand, but they weren't the ones who had been the victim of the Wests. How could they have understood?

After giving my new statement, I wanted to go home but I had to stay and be interviewed by another detective who had come down from Gloucester to question me.

A big fair-haired man, built like a rugby player, came into the interview room and introduced himself as DC Smith. (Not his real name.) He looked me up and down, then took the statement and left the room.

A policewoman brought me a cup of tea while I waited for him to return. She was very nice to me and asked if I was all right and did I want her to get my mum to come down? I told her that I didn't want my mum with me, as I didn't want to hurt her with all the details; I knew she wouldn't be able to cope with it all.

Ten minutes later, DC Smith came back into the room and looked at me in a way that made me feel uncomfortable. The policewoman stayed and DC Jones stood in the corner watching as DC Smith started asking me questions. I had to explain, again, why I had not mentioned the rape in the first statement. Then he asked me to tell him a bit about myself. What my family life was like.

I told him how I didn't get on too well with Alf or Phillip, but that I got on OK with the rest of the kids; that I was often accused of being Mum's favourite and that I loved my mum a lot.

Then he asked me what kind of things I liked to do. I told him I liked dancing and discos and horse riding, writing to my pen pals, writing poetry and motorbikes.

Then he asked me about Tony. How had I met him? What was my relationship with Tony like? Did I love him? I told him I loved Tony, but I didn't think he loved me as much, if at all.

He asked me how many boyfriends I'd had. I told him that I had had three steady ones and a few shorter-term ones.

Then he asked me how many lovers I'd had. As soon as he asked that question, I blushed.

I looked at DC Jones and asked, 'Do I really have to answer that question?'

He nodded and said, 'Yes, I'm afraid so.'

I could feel myself burning up and the tears began to fall in torrents from my eyes. I didn't want to tell them about all the men I had been with. I was already ashamed of my past, but I had no choice. I asked if my stepfather and Mum would have to know what I was about to tell them and they said 'no'.

I told them about some of the men I'd been with, but not all. I didn't mention the attempted rape at Cromwell Street. I wanted to but I knew they would think I was a slut. I wished more than ever that my mum had not gone to the police.

Then DC Smith leaned over the table, his face close to mine, and said, 'What about Ben Stanniland? What about the other visitors to the house?' Then he added, 'You had sex with both of them, didn't you?'

I felt like I was the accused. I felt ashamed and humiliated and put my head down and cried.

He then went on and on about the night I had spent in the lodgers' room.

'Do you take drugs, do you use cannabis? Do you like getting drunk? Do you enjoy sex?' He continually bombarded me with questions, hardly giving me time to answer one before going on to the next.

Then he asked about Steve Riddall, my sailor boyfriend. In a brutal way, he said, 'You had sex with him at Cromwell Street too, didn't you?'

'Yes, yes I did. So what, what has that got to do with what the Wests did to me?' I yelled at him.

He retorted, 'You like threesomes, don't you?'

'No! I've never been in a threesome!' I cried back. I was getting angry and frustrated; he wasn't listening to me. 'I wasn't in a threesome. It wasn't like you're saying,' I angrily blasted back at him.

His voice had become louder as he boomed, 'You enjoy sex, don't you, Caroline? You were willing to go along with what the Wests wanted, weren't you? You wanted it – didn't you? What happened, did they go too far for your liking – is that why you decided to report them?'

All the time, he was right in my face as he accused me of all these things, all these lies. I hated him; I felt he was enjoying himself at my expense. He was no better than the Wests. He was painting me out to be some sort of Jezebel!

I wished at that moment that the Wests had killed me – it would have been a merciful release from the hell that DC Smith was putting me through. This barrage of questions, his heavy-handedness into this inquiry and his bullying barrack-room interrogation style of interviewing had left me feeling ashamed.

I knew I hadn't been the most innocent of victims, but I didn't deserve this. DC Smith stood and grinned at me as he thanked me and left the room, leaving me to cry and to ponder on his not-very-adept handling of the situation.

At first, the young policewoman looked uncomfortable, then she asked if I would like another cup of tea. I told her I just wanted to go home. (In fact, at that precise moment, I didn't want to go home, I just wanted to kill myself. I felt I would never be able to face my family ever again. I felt like a dirty bitch, a slag that deserved everything she got.)

The policewoman, seeing me in distress, said, 'I'll go and see if you can go.'

She came back and said DC Jones needed to have a word with me.

A rather embarrassed DC Jones came back into the room and sat next to me. He said that DC Smith had been to interview Fred and Rose and they had, at first, denied all charges of indecent assault. A search of their car was carried out and they found the button that had come off my trousers.

When the police put the rape charge to the Wests, they said they were willing to admit to indecent assault, but that no rape had taken place and that I would have to face up to them in court.

'I'm afraid you will be questioned about your personal life, in a similar way to how DC Smith behaved,' DC Jones said.

I lowered my head and cried. 'I can't go through that again.

I'm sorry but I'm not going to court! Will I have to go if they've pleaded guilty to the indecent assault?'

DC Jones said, 'No, but you'll be letting them get away with what they've done.'

I continued my crying as I said, 'I don't care, I'm not going to court, they will still be put away for what they've done, won't they? After all, they kidnapped me and attacked me. That should get them locked up, shouldn't it?'

'Not necessarily,' DC Jones replied.

I stood up and said, 'I want to go now, can I go? I'm tired.'

'We'll be in touch, soon. Think about it carefully, you really should go to court,' DC Jones said as he walked me to the door.

'I will,' I said, knowing in my heart that nothing would make me go through that ordeal again. The fear of the stigma attached to a court appearance only added to what I was going through.

I didn't go home straight away. I went down to the Globe pub and got very drunk. Then I went home to bed.

Later that evening, when I got up, I could sense a change of atmosphere in the house. Phillip was trying to avoid me. He looked embarrassed, but not in a nasty way. It was as if he felt sorry for me and didn't know how to handle it.

Alf asked me if I would have to go to court. Maybe I was being paranoid, but I felt he was more concerned about what his friends and neighbours would think as opposed to what I had been through. I told him I would not be going to court and left it at that.

Sue, my sister, wanted to know more about what had happened, though I knew she had already pestered Mum to death on the subject and Mum had told all the family and some close neighbours what had happened.

Things in the house were different; there were no fights and arguments. No one was sarcastic; it was like everyone was walking on eggshells for fear of upsetting me. I felt like a guest in my own home. It was too weird for me to handle, so I spent as much time as possible with my mate Julie O'Shea.

We went for walks or sat in her bedroom most evenings. It was hard for Julie too – she was used to me being full of life and laughter. I tried to keep my 'happy face' on for her, but she could see through me, and now and then we would both end up in tears.

I couldn't sleep properly. I was having nightmares about that night and kept searching for a way out. A lot of *if onlys* went through my mind, even in my nightmares. Eventually, I told the police that I would not go to court; I would not press the rape charge.

I felt awful, as if I had wasted police time, but I could not do it. The fewer people who knew about what kind of girl I was, the better. DC Smith thought I had enjoyed it. Alf, and I imagined most of the people on the estate, felt I had asked for it.

I didn't talk about it to anyone; as far as I was concerned it was over. And the least said the quicker it would be forgotten by others. As for me, I would never forget what had happened or how I felt about myself.

I did have some very good female friends who I used to be able to talk to, but that all changed after the Wests. I no longer trusted my girlfriends. Things had altered. I couldn't try on clothes with them or get changed for swimming without using a cubicle to cover my body from their eyes in case they fancied me or tried it on with me.

I also worried that they thought I was a lesbian. After what the Wests did to me I had no one to talk to, not even Mum – it would have hurt her too much.

My relationship with Tony also changed after the Wests attacked me. At first, I still hitchhiked to see him, but after a lorry driver tried to kiss me I decided I couldn't take the risk any more.

The Wests went to trial and got away with a slap on the wrist and a fine. The report in the *Citizen* on 13 January 1973 made it seem as though I had co-operated with them and had not tried to help myself. I felt like I was in the wrong – yet again.

I wanted to forget all about the Wests and all the things connected to them, including Tony, who I felt at the time was not supportive enough. I felt Alf and DC Smith had both believed that I was a willing participant in what the Wests had done to me and now even the judge seemed to agree with them. I knew it wasn't true, but there was nothing I could do to change what had happened so I tried to forget it – and embarked on a merry-go-round of self-destruction.

8

THE JINX

WITHIN DAYS OF the trial, I started drinking heavily to numb my memory. When I went out socialising, I drank even more just to give me the confidence to talk to people.

I would dance till I dropped and drink on till I threw up. I slept around and took on a string of lovers; this was in order to prove to myself and everyone else that I was not a lesbian or some kind of freak. The remarks Fred and Rose had made about my genitals had left a scar too. Yet none of my lovers had mentioned that I was different in any way to other girls they had slept with.

The men that stayed I would treat appallingly. Forever seeing how far I could push and goad them, I would hit them in temper and let fly regardless of what they dished out to me in return. I was always testing their love for me and when I pushed them too far, they would leave me and I would hate myself for the way I had behaved towards them.

On Friday 13 April 1973, I met my next boyfriend, Sean, a lovely gentle giant from Northern Ireland. His family had moved back to the Forest of Dean because of the Troubles. We had been seeing each other for about a month when Alf called me into the living room and said, 'Your boyfriend was on the news programme, he's been arrested for murder.' Sean had shot a policeman in Ireland and was revealed to be a member of the IRA. I couldn't believe it – he had seemed such a lovely person, quiet and gentle. Sean served fourteen years in the Maze Prison. During those fourteen years, I wrote to him and I even went over to visit him in 1985. I didn't condone his crime, but I didn't judge him either. As far as he was concerned, he was at war and was classed as a political prisoner.

After Sean, I went out with a boy called Dave from a nearby village. Dave would come up to see me on his 125cc motorbike – I called it a 'hair dryer' as I liked the bigger bikes. One night, shortly after we had started dating, Dave and I had an argument and by the time we had made up, Dave ended up going home an hour later than usual. It was pub closing time, and a drunk hit-and-run driver mowed Dave off his bike and left him to lie on the road with a broken arm and two breaks in his leg. Dave spent several months in hospital.

Meanwhile, a face from the past came back on the scene. One night, Tony, who by now had passed his driving test, picked me up and took me back to Tewkesbury. We went to a disco and while we were there some bikers came in and started causing trouble. I saw Tony go up to one of them and tell him to cool it or get out.

Then I saw the biker, the one who Tony had words with,

throw what I thought were two punches at Tony, twice in the body then turn and run out of the building. Tony chased after him and I followed him outside. Tony caught up with the biker, grabbed him by the throat and pushed him against the wall. Then, slowly, Tony fell to the ground and the biker and his mates ran off. Tony was muttering, 'Get him,' then blacked out. I saw blood on his shirt and lifted it, only to find out that he had been stabbed in the stomach and the chest.

Usually I would have been sick at the sight, but somehow I managed to keep calm for Tony's sake. Two of Tony's friends picked him up and as they did I could see Tony's intestines protruding out of his stomach wound. I held them in place while his friends carried him the 200 yards to the hospital.

Tony had to have a life-saving operation and stayed in hospital for two months. After that, I didn't see him again, just the odd phone call.

By now I was convinced I was a jinx.

A few months later, Dave and I got back together, but it was a very on–off relationship. I was two-timing him on several occasions and we would split up for weeks at a time. I was exceedingly jealous of Dave and accused him of two-timing me all the time, but I guess it was the guilt over my own infidelity that made me accuse him.

In October 1974, on my nineteenth birthday, I saw my dad for the first time in ten years. I was so happy that he wanted to see me, and when Michael told me he had got married and that I had a younger sister and brother, I became very excited at the prospect of meeting them and told him so. My excitement was short lived. My dad told me that I would not be meeting them.

He told me he was going back to Southern Ireland with his family in the near future.

I asked if I could write to him now and then. His reply was like a slap in the face: 'No, you won't be able to write to me. You see, my wife and family don't know about you and Phillip.'

He gave me a gold watch for my birthday, then walked out of my life for the very last time. I was left with the feeling that he was ashamed of my existence. I was his dark secret, the living proof of his sins against the Catholic Church, of which he was a respected member. This was my father, the man whom I had taken many a beating for while defending his absence.

I made up excuses as to why he couldn't look after me. I rejected Alf as a father and all the time it seemed Alf had been right – my father would not be coming back for me.

My father did not want me. Mum knew how hurt I felt; she felt it too, of course. My father, by denying my existence, had also erased her time with him – and she had always loved him.

I was left with a bitter taste in my mouth. Inside I had to admit that I owed Alf an apology and a big thank-you for struggling to bring me up. I didn't say anything to Alf – how could I? I was too proud and too afraid of having my apology rejected – but my feelings towards him changed the day my father left for good. I don't know if Alf ever knew what had happened, but I'm sure he noticed that I was less cocky and argumentative towards him.

In 1976, after putting up with me for nearly three years, Dave ended our relationship. Unable to accept this rejection, I moved away to work as a chambermaid at the Rozel Hotel in Weston-

Super-Mare. I soon got into the club-and-drinks scene and set myself hurtling further down the path of self-destruction.

I got myself another boyfriend – the town stud, who was only out for what he could get. When he finished with me, after a month or so, I went further downhill fast and ended up on anti-depressants. At the age of twenty, life was too painful for me to deal with and, at my lowest, I decided to end it all and swallowed the entire bottle of pills.

I ended up in hospital having my stomach pumped. A psychiatrist saw me and told me I was suffering from a fear of rejection from men, which started for the first time when my real father left me as a child. The psychiatrist told me that I should write down my fears and feelings, both good and bad, and that it would be a therapy for me. I had been keeping diaries since 1973, but had never put my feelings down in them, as I was afraid of someone reading them, so I got a notebook and poured my heart out into it.

On a bad day, I would read about a good day and it would lift me up out of the depression for a while. To a certain degree, it did work but I still didn't let everything out for fear of snooping eyes discovering my innermost secret thoughts.

I moved back home to Cinderford, back to my mum. My suicide attempt had really scared her and she made me promise never to try to kill myself again. Seeing the tears in her eyes as she spoke made me realise that no man was worth dying for – not because I valued myself in any way, but because I didn't want to see my mum hurt like that again.

9

CARNIVAL QUEEN

AT THE AGE of 21, I had a new boyfriend – Kim, a tall shy boy of 18 from Woodside Avenue, the nice area of Cinderford. I don't think his dad approved of me, having learned of my reputation, but Kim's mother was a lovely lady and always made me feel welcome. I was still suffering from low self-esteem, so I preferred to stay in with Kim, either babysitting his little sister or helping him to do up his old car. I didn't like going out with him, as I worried I might feel jealous and start picking on him about girls we saw or passed. I always believed that he would prefer to be with them rather than me.

We had started seeing each other in November 1976; by June 1977 I was treating Kim as badly as I had Dave. I even became jealous of him watching pretty girls on TV. *Top of the Pops* was a nightmare for both of us to watch together. I would always have to make a snide and sarcastic comment about Pan's People, the glamorous, scantily dressed dancing troupe that wore sexy clothes. It would really upset me to see him looking at them when I felt so ugly, short, dumpy and flat-chested in comparison to them. I was slim and pretty, but I didn't see myself that way at the time. I hated myself on the inside, I hated my jealousy and I hated the way I abused Kim. I still felt that everyone would be better off if I was dead. If it hadn't been for Mum, I would have taken another overdose – the easy way out.

In 1977, Mum suggested I enter the Cinderford Carnival Queen Contest. I was not too keen on doing so, but Mum insisted it would prove to me that I was attractive. All contestants had to have their photographs taken. These were then put in the local *Mercury* newspaper and the public voted for the girl of their choice.

To my surprise, I made it to the final, which was held at the Woodlands Hotel. Ten of us had to walk in front of the judges and we were asked about our hobbies (dancing and horse riding in my case) and ourselves. I hated the sound of my voice, which I could hear being transmitted through the giant speakers. I sounded just like one of the West Country singing group The Wurzels. I couldn't help feeling that I must be coming across as really boring, but I put on my 'happy face' … and, somehow, I won!

I felt so proud when Cinderford's mayor, Frank Beard, crowned me Miss Royal Forest of Dean Carnival & Trades Queen, though I was soon dragged back down to earth when I overheard one of the contestants moaning to her mother that the contest must have been fixed.

Winning was supposed to help me with my confidence and self-esteem, but I still didn't like myself and later I didn't carry out any official duties after the initial opening of the Cinderford Carnival. I felt like I wasn't really there as I waved to the crowds of people who were lining the route of the parade up through the High Street and down past the police station to Lister's Recreation Ground.

The organisers gave speeches and the mayor introduced me to the huge crowd. I was shaking from head to toe, inside and out, as I walked towards the dreaded microphone. I stood there on a platform facing the crowd of locals reading out my short 'Thank You' speech. It should have been a proud moment for me, but all the time I was convinced that the crowd thought I was nothing but a cheap slut. Men that I'd slept with and girls that had bullied me in the past mingled in the crowd.

There were people who knew I had been raped, some of whom I remembered had been gossiping about me four years earlier when the Wests' court case was reported in the Gloucester *Citizen*. This tittle-tattle overshadowed my occasion.

The judge's words in that court case stuck in my mind – that during the assault there must have been some passive co-operation on my part. Add to that the fact that the Wests had only been fined £25 each for each of the charges against them, and a total of £100 was all that I was worth. No prison sentence, just a slapped wrist and the advice to seek psychiatric help! The judge must have thought that the Wests couldn't have been that evil, or else they wouldn't have kept giving me cups of tea. Four years had passed, but it was all still raw in my mind, and because I hadn't forgot it I felt the gossips, with their idle chit-chat, hadn't forgotten it either. I felt I was left with a 'scarlet woman' tag that was difficult to shake off.

Looking back, I realise that those 'gossips' had no reason to remember that newspaper cutting, which I had destroyed immediately after reading it. I had burned it so no one else would read it. I felt that if I destroyed the evidence then it would be easier to forget, but it wasn't easy to forget, not for me. The gossip-mongerers had most likely gone on to the next bit of gossip the following week, but in my mind I felt they all remembered it as well as I did. I felt they were looking down on me, sniggering to each other about me as they passed the word around through the crowd to those who were unaware of my past, my shame.

I must have been suffering from paranoia, but didn't know it as I stood on that stage in my finery looking every bit the Queen of the Carnival. All those faces in the crowd looking up at me, smiling at me and applauding me. Yet in my head they were all being two-faced and I convinced myself that they didn't think I was anything special.

One man, though, thought I was special and he approached me at a later date after seeing my photograph in the *Western Daily Press* and the *Citizen*. The man asked if I would be interested in doing some photographic modelling for him. Modelling had been my second dream career when I had left school, after being a children's nanny. I wondered whether if I said 'yes' to his offer, I would end up being humiliated again. I took his contact number but decided to put his offer on hold for a while.

By August 1978, Kim and I had made it through another year, but only just; we were off and on all the time. I was still consumed with jealousy and was suspicious of what he was getting up to at college. I was even jealous of the nights he stayed in revising for his exams. I was jealous of the time he spent learning judo and the female family friend he trained with.

I could tell he was going off me, big time. I felt abandoned when Kim went abroad on holiday with his family and his cousin, who was the same age as him. I couldn't sleep and I couldn't concentrate at work, as jealous thoughts were racing around my mind.

I imagined Kim being with other girls, laughing and enjoying their company, having sex with them and telling them he didn't have a girlfriend back home. Jealousy was eating away at me.

The first week that Kim was away I stayed in, being a good girlfriend. By the second week I was driving myself crazy with my vile imagination, so when two friends, V and S, asked me out, I went.

We went to a disco at a local pub and got very drunk. V was seeing an older married man who still played the field. S had been going out with Bob (not his real name) for a couple of weeks. Bob lost his only child to a cot death; he invited us back to his place for supper and to watch a film on TV.

I didn't particularly like this immoral group of men, as they were sleazy married womanisers. I only went along because my friends had said they wouldn't stay long. There was one decent younger man with them whom I got on with, so I thought I'd stick close to him. We bought a Chinese take-away, made coffee and sat down to watch TV.

Soon after we got there, V and her boyfriend, the married man, disappeared upstairs into a bedroom. I was half expecting this to happen, but hoped they wouldn't be long. I went to the toilet and when I got back the nice lad had gone and I was left downstairs with Terry (not his real name), also a married man. By this time, S and Bob were getting very carried away in front of us.

Terry said, 'I can't sit here watching them two, I'm going to sit in the spare bedroom, you coming?'

I told him I would be going home soon, followed him up the stairs and knocked on the bedroom door that V and her boyfriend were in.

I shouted, 'V, are you coming home now? It's getting late.'

'Yeah, give me five minutes,' she shouted back through the door.

I sat on the top step and waited. It was obvious from the sounds coming from the room that V was nowhere near ready to leave!

Terry invited me to sit on the bed with him but I declined, telling him we would be going soon.

'Nah, you won't,' he said, 'They are there for the night now.'

I knew he was right and I hated V for being so selfish. She knew I wouldn't walk home on my own and she had said we wouldn't be staying there long.

I didn't really want to be alone with Terry, as he had a reputation and had a nasty streak in him. He was another man who thought he was God's gift to women, but in my eyes he was a disgusting overweight slob and a philanderer.

Reluctantly, I entered the bedroom. He began talking to me about a very personal matter, and showed me a side I didn't know he had. His gentle tone lured me into a false sense of security and I sat down on the edge of the bed while he lay down.

'You might as well get some rest,' he said as he moved over. I reluctantly laid down with my back to him.

After about ten minutes, he pulled me round to him and tried to kiss me.

'Oh, don't start, just go to sleep, will you?' I said. I tried to say it in a firm but non-aggressive way; I didn't want to upset him in case he got nasty. I tried not to panic even though I was worried.

'Just give me one kiss and I'll leave you alone,' he said.

Rather foolishly, I gave him one kiss, after which I said, 'Right, that's it, now go to sleep.'

With that, he grabbed me roughly, my face squeezed in his one hand. The other hand, in a fist, was raised above my face ready to strike me. 'You don't fucking tease me and get away with it, bitch, do as you're told or you'll get this,' he growled as he pushed his fist closer towards my face.

Nodding at his fist, I lay there still and silent till it was over, too scared to call for help, too shocked that this should be happening to me on a repeat basis. Again, I was in the wrong place with the wrong person, giving the wrong impression.

When he had finished, he rolled over on his back and said cockily, 'Now you know what a real man's like, not like that airy-fairy young lad you're used to.' He seemed completely oblivious to the fact that he had just raped me. I felt so sick and so angry with him, and with V, but I was mostly angry with myself for yet again putting myself in such a vulnerable situation. Later that day, I heard, Terry was in the pub bragging to all his mates that he'd 'had the Carnival Queen'.

It never even crossed my mind to go to the police – I

couldn't have proved anything, it would have only added to my humiliation. I was still smarting from the previous rape and the way the police had mistreated me.

I decided I would get my revenge by telling his wife and, hopefully, break up his marriage. I actually sat down and wrote his wife a letter telling her what he had done to me and about all the affairs he'd had. I put the letter in an envelope and put a stamp on it, but I couldn't bring myself to send it. My conscience got the better of me. I was told that he was very abusive to his wife – she didn't need me adding to her misery too.

When Kim came back from holiday, I tried my best not to question him too much or get jealous. When he started back at college, I noticed that he had changed towards me; his feelings towards me had cooled off. He spent more time with his mates, lunchtimes in the pub, trips in the evenings, ice-skating and discos in Bristol.

He wouldn't take any crap from me any more, no emotional blackmail, no mind games – they didn't work any more. He'd had enough of my jealousy and possessiveness. If we did row, it had to be me that did all of the running to make it up, not Kim.

One night, when I was feeling particularly upset, I blurted out to Kim that Terry was a rapist. Kim wet out looking for him and shouted out in front of his mates that he was a rapist. I was proud of Kim – he wasn't a tough guy, he was a gentle man, and that took a lot of courage. There weren't many men who would have stood up to Terry.

10

TEASE

IN NOVEMBER 1978, I popped into the college canteen to see Kim. He wasn't expecting me; I made some lame excuse about having to tell him something that couldn't wait. When I found him, I could see he was nervous and embarrassed about me being there. A young girl walked in and smiled at him. I felt she was just about to walk up to him – then, seeing me, she changed direction and went up to his mate instead. I knew straight away that she was seeing Kim. Later that night, I confronted Kim with my suspicions. He told me she was his mate's friend and that he didn't fancy her and didn't know her, except to say hello to.

The following week, I bumped into her at the local rugby club disco and asked her if she was seeing my boyfriend. Of course, she denied it. She said she had a boyfriend, an older married man. She stayed chatting to me for a while and suggested we have a girls' night out sometime. I put my suspicions to the backburner of my mind, but no matter how hard I tried to suffocate the thoughts of Kim two-timing me, they kept sneaking back to the front of my mind, haunting me with doubt.

I was losing the fight with my jealousy and one night in December, I spat out all my pent-up anger and accusations at Kim and we had another huge row. I couldn't hold back any longer after the questioning, the cross-examining, trying to trick him into letting something slip out, something that would prove my suspicions were right. As I got out of the car, I could see Kim was in tears. He'd had all he could take of his 'sicko' girlfriend.

The next day, I phoned him to say sorry and asked him to come and see me for half an hour, but he said he had college work to get through. I whined on and he gave in – as usual. I got into his car and we drove into the woods and parked up. This was the place we did most of our love-making – our Lovers' Lane. I asked for a kiss but Kim avoided any intimacy and said he had something to tell me. I could tell by the expression on his face that I was not going to like what he had to say.

Kim tried to finish with me, saying his college work was suffering because of me. I told him I would leave him to get on with it and not see him two days of the week, but he had heard all of that before. I always ended up wanting to see him, keeping on at him until he gave in.

In the end, he told me the truth: he didn't want to see me any more because he didn't love me any more. I didn't believe him: he *must* love me; he couldn't suddenly *not* love me! Feelings don't change overnight! I promised him that I would change; I would do anything he wanted, as long as he didn't leave me. Kim was having none of it; he said he had made up his mind and that he couldn't cope with me any more. It was over.

I was absolutely devastated, the bottom had fallen out of my world – yet again.

It is with overwhelming shame and disgust that I have to admit at this point I sank to my all-time lowest. I lashed out at Kim, beating him, punching and scramming at his face. I was ranting, screaming, telling him he could not end it.

Then I threatened to kill myself; or I would kill him. I begged him to make love to me; he refused. He had never been able to turn down sex with me before, and with this I felt I had lost my hold on him. I couldn't take the rejection.

'Just one last time,' I pleaded with him.

'No!' he replied.

At that point, I lost all self-control and tried to force him to have sex with me. If I couldn't have Kim, I felt, I wanted his child: that way I would always have a part of him.

I was like a woman possessed – groping at him, trying to get him erect, forcing myself on him and forcing my kisses on him. Being the gentle lad he was, he just held me away from him. Not saying anything. Just waiting for me to come to my senses. And when I did, I sank back in my seat in misery and cried and cried. Not just for myself, but also for what I had done to Kim. I was no better than all the people who had assaulted or raped me.

I felt so sorry for Kim. I hated myself for what I had done to him, not just that night but throughout the two years we were together. As I got out of the car that night, I was choking back my tears, choking on my words. I said, 'I'm so sorry, I'm so very sorry, Kim. I won't ever bother you again, I promise.' And I meant it.

After that, I never wanted a steady relationship ever again. As far as I was concerned, I was evil. I was sick in the mind. I was sick of my jealousy. It destroyed everything that was good in my life; it was soul destroying. Once again, I wished I was dead. The world would be a better place without me.

11

A NEW LIFE

I MANAGED TO stay away from Kim by hanging out with the hippy crowd of the town – older men who were into Bruce Springsteen, Frank Zappa … and drugs. I knew they smoked cannabis and I started off having the occasional puff on a joint when we went back to one or the other's house after the pubs had closed. Then I was introduced to speed (amphetamine sulphate) and I loved it. Speed gave me confidence; it numbed my feelings of self-hate, it made me chatty and bubbly and, in my mind, popular.

I made contact with the photographer who had approached me at the carnival and had some test shots done. I started getting some modelling work for amateur photographers that paid £10 an hour. I started off in lingerie then, reluctantly, moved on to glamour (topless). I was surprised that anyone would want to photograph me topless, as I only had small breasts at the time, and I was quite self-conscious about my boobs. But I made myself a promise that I would never do anything rude, like pretend to touch myself, as I didn't want to be that kind of model. I began modelling work in my spare time and worked at Cinderford Engineering as my main bread-and-butter job.

I started smoking cannabis during the daytime and taking speed on the weekends so that I could go out and party all night. It wasn't long before I was losing time from my day job, because I was always tired during the week. I made up my money by modelling two or three hours a week – it earned me as much as a week's pay from the factory. I hated the factory work, it was dirty and boring; modelling was hard work but glamorous, it made me feel good about myself.

I started seeing a local man called Greg. It wasn't love – I didn't even like him that much – it was a rebound affair. I saw Greg so as to stop me thinking of Kim. Once I got into the drugs scene I soon realised it was a big mistake and I finished with Greg.

I had a few boyfriends on the go at once for a couple of weeks, and then Kim came back on the scene. I had found out from a friend that Kim had been two-timing me, which confirmed my suspicion about him being unfaithful and convinced me that it hadn't all been in my imagination. Towards the end of our two years together, he had finished with me to be with Nicola, the girl he had met at college.

Kim came to see me on the pretence of returning some of my things, things that I didn't really want back. I think he was overwhelmed by the change in me and by how happy and bubbly I was. The old Caroline was back, the one he had first fallen in love with. There were no questions, no jealousy, no pleading for him to come back to me and no accusations about his two-timing me. (He didn't know that it was the cannabis joint I had smoked before he showed up that had relaxed me!)

I showed Kim some of my modelling photographs and he was well impressed. Even Alf took an interest in these photos – he had always liked girlie magazines; he and his mates would swap them. Alf showed some of his friends my pictures too. It was strange for me to see that Alf was proud of something I had done, something that most fathers would have been upset about. I put this exuberance down to the fact that I was not his biological daughter. It wasn't till years later that a counsellor suggested to me that maybe the reason Alf was so nasty to me at times was because it was a way of him protecting me from his sexual feelings towards me.

Being the bitch that I was, I started a sexual relationship with Kim behind Nicola's back. He would see me two or three times a week for a month. By now, I had convinced myself that I was using him and getting revenge on Nicola for taking him away from me. In reality, he was using me. I was still in love with him. I asked him to stop seeing Nicola and make a go of things with me, but he wouldn't so I finished it. I threw myself into the modelling and the drugs and I forgot about Kim … for a while.

I decided to get on with my life and make a go of my modelling – it would be my passport out of Cinderford and away from all the painful memories it held for me. I knew I was getting out of my depth with the drugs and my promiscuous behaviour. The promiscuity took place when I was under the influence of drugs. I was getting a really bad reputation as a harlot. I thought I was in control, but I wasn't. I wasn't popular. I was an easy lay – that's why I had so many admirers. I wanted the chance to start over again, somewhere new, where no one knew me, where I could find the real me, not the 'happy face' or the 'hard face', but the real me.

I sent a portfolio of my photos to Kay's catalogue and was accepted to model for them. I was so excited, full of dreams and aspirations of what a good future I had ahead of me, I was so happy. My happiness was soon dashed against the rock of despair, however, when days later I discovered I was pregnant!

When Dr Gadsby told me the news, I cried, 'Oh, no! I can't be pregnant, not now!' I think this surprised him. He was used to me asking for a pregnancy test – my periods were very erratic, always late – but the results were always negative. I guess he suspected that I longed for a baby.

I explained my predicament to the doctor. I could not believe my bad luck. I was torn in two: my dream of fame and the good life were pulling me one way; the baby – I felt sure it was Kim's – was pulling me in the opposite direction. Any other time, I would have been over the moon that I was expecting a baby, but at that precise time I had other dreams and needs.

Dr Gadsby was fairly new to the area. He was only a little older than me and very laid back. I found him easy to talk to. He knew of my past depression and attempted suicide; I even told him that I had been taking illegal drugs and that I was worried they may have affected the baby inside me. I hated the thought of having an abortion, it was wrong, but I also hated the idea of losing out on my big chance to change my life for the better.

We talked about the possibility of my postponing the modelling career for a year and having the baby. Dr Gadsby knew I wouldn't have coped with the guilt and the emotional turmoil of having an abortion – he summed it all up for me in one sentence when he said, 'I think having this baby would be good for you – you need someone to love, someone to love you; it would give you a reason to live.' He was right.

He told me to go home and talk to my mum, and give it some deep thought before making a decision, which I did. I told my mum the news and she sympathised with me, but she said it was my choice. She said she would help me out with babysitting if I wanted to do modelling or get a job, but she never tried to influence my decision. The next time I saw Dr Gadsby I was smiling all over my face and I thanked him for helping me to do the right thing for all concerned.

I phoned Kim to tell him I was expecting his child. At first, he was dumbstruck. Then he told me he didn't think it was his baby, as he knew I had been sleeping around. His words made me so angry that I threatened to have blood tests done when the baby was born to prove he was the father.

When I was eight weeks pregnant, a fourteen-year-old local boy attacked me in Belle Vue Road, in Cinderford. He had been flashing at me! As he got nearer to me, I told him to behave and cover himself up, or I would tell his dad. I thought it would make him feel silly and he would leave me alone, but instead he grabbed me, telling me he was going to 'shag' me. He tried to drag me behind the library wall, but I managed to fight him off. I reported him to the police and it went to trial later in the year.

The boy's father decided to cover up for him and said that the boy was with him at home at the time of the assault. His father also tried to get in touch with me to try and persuade me to drop the charges and, as a consequence, I had to have police protection. I moved out, temporarily, to avoid him.

When the case finally went to court in the November, the boy was found 'not guilty'. I lost all faith in the justice system. My biker friends, who were then known as the Desperados, had offered to dish out their own brand of justice, but I declined their offer. I hoped the boy was just going through the hormonal stages of puberty and that he would be too scared to do anything like that again.

In the meantime, I kept my pregnancy a secret from Alf – I thought he would call me names and throw me out if he found out. Instead, when he found out from someone outside of the family when I was four months on, in my eyes he became a father to me for the first time ever. There was no big shouting match full of accusations that I'd been behaving like a tart. Instead, he talked softly to me about what I wanted to do about the baby. He said he would help me out.

There wasn't enough room at our house, so Alf said he would get on to the council for me and tell them we were overcrowded so they would give me a flat. Until then, he told me I could have the best room to myself and turn it into my bedroom. I was very humbled by Alf's unexpected attitude towards me and felt even guiltier about the verbal abuse I had inflicted upon him over the years. It was so nice that we were actually being civil to each other.

Once again, however, just as I was starting to feel happy my luck was to change.

One night, I had been violently sick; the baby's heartbeat was so faint that my doctor ordered me to take bed rest. During that time, Alf suffered another heart attack and was rushed into Gloucester Royal Hospital and kept in. A week later, I was well enough to go and see him. When I set eyes on Alf, he looked so frail; he was trying to be chirpy but he was in a bad way. He had fallen out of his hospital bed and broken a couple of ribs and was very uncomfortable.

I felt so sorry for all the bad-mouthing I had given him over the years. He was my dad, in the true sense of the word, and always had been ever since he took me on as a four-year-old. He was the one that fed me, sheltered me and dressed me and all I had done to repay him was to rebel against everything he asked of me.

I now realised that, in all that time, I had a dad in Alf. In reality, Michael was just someone that my mum had loved and who had gone on to make her pregnant. To Michael, I was only ever a deep, dark secret.

On my visit to the hospital, I told Alf I would be back on the Sunday to see him, but he just gave me a smile and said, 'I'll be off up Jacob's ladder that day.' I gave him a hug (for the first time ever), laughed and told him, 'You're too wicked to be going off up there.' He obviously knew something we didn't though and, true to his word, Alf died on the morning of Sunday 7 October 1979. I was six months' pregnant at the time.

I was so devastated by his death. Once again the 'happy face' that I used to protect myself when I felt hurt slipped in place. I felt my family would think I was just after some attention if I cried alongside them. They were so used to Alf and me hating each other and being at each other's throats that I figured they would never believe that I was hurting as much, if not more, than they were. I dealt with the bereavement by keeping busy; I spring-cleaned the house upstairs while they grieved together downstairs.

After the funeral, all family and friends went back to the house, but I didn't feel like I could so I met up with a crowd of men friends of mine from the Northern Strip Mine and got so drunk that I started throwing up all over the place. I eventually passed out and was taken to a friend's to sleep it off.

On 24 January 1980, at the age of 24, I gave birth to my daughter Kelly. She was born at the local Dilke Hospital, which meant she was classed as a Forester. As a true Forester, she even had rights: she could let her sheep graze freely anywhere in the Forest of Dean and/or become a Free Miner and dig her own coal! Kelly would never have wanted to use that right, but it was something the Foresters were proud of. In Gloucester, Foresters were often referred to as 'sheep shaggers' and were thought to be a little backward; maybe that was because of the heavy Forest twang. For years, I thought they were calling me 'Albert' till I realised it was the Foresters' word for 'my old friend' or 'my old buddy' – 'How be you, albut?' or 'All right o' butty?' I had problems with the drawl to begin with, but soon found myself talking with it too – 'Ooh, arh!'

When Kelly was three months old, I was given a one-bedroom council flat in Hilldene, not far from my mum's. I was sad that Alf had never seen or held Kelly, 'cause she was so sweet. He would have found it easy to love her.

I had been convinced Kelly was Kim's baby, but the blood

tests proved me wrong: it turned out that Greg was her father! My periods were so hit and miss, I'd had a period after Greg and I had finished, then I started seeing Kim, but it seems I had one more period after conceiving. I was devastated by the results of the tests; I felt like I'd been cheated. But I still loved Kelly more than anything else in my life.

As she grew older, she came to resemble Greg more and more. At first, he had denied her; in time we came to the understanding that he was her father, but he didn't want to take on that role. Another generation, another little girl without the love and nurturing of her father, another little girl rejected and hurt by it. I feel responsible for that, just as my mum felt responsible for me being without my father.

I felt bad that Kelly's dad didn't want anything to do with her; he had a new girlfriend and didn't want to be involved in Kelly's upbringing. I felt sorry for my baby girl not having a dad, but she would always have a mum.

Being a mum changed everything for me. I knew for certain that, no matter how bad life became, I would never consider killing myself again, not as long as Kelly was alive to care for. Kelly was my life, my girl, my life-saver.

12

ROCK 'N' ROLL

WHEN KELLY WAS six months old, I got a job as a barmaid in a local pub, the Golden Lion. They had bands playing there four times a week and all my friends would go there, but I couldn't afford a night out. So by working there I was able to see my mates, see all the bands, earn a few quid to subsidise my benefits and give my mum some money to babysit Kelly.

While working there, I befriended all the bands and even got to sing now and then when they had jamming sessions. At these spontaneous sessions, anyone could get up and join in with the unrehearsed music, mixing with musicians from all the different bands playing together. During one of these impromptu get-togethers I met a musician named Dick. I was five years younger than Dick, which made a change from my usual younger boyfriends.

A string of female admirers adored being around Dick, but

that didn't put me off – nor did the fact that he had a pregnant girlfriend! I turned on the charm and pursued him till I got him. He told me it was all over between him and his girlfriend long before I came on the scene. I believed him; I wanted to believe him, even though deep down I thought that they could have made a go of things if I wasn't on the scene. Yet again, I was being a bitch!

I let Dick move in with us; he stayed for twelve months. During the time I was with Dick, he taught me to sing and write lyrics and I even went on a mini-tour, fronting the band we had put together, singing my own songs with a few Motown and Rod Stewart songs thrown in to get the audience dancing. I loved it, but I was still too shy to stand up in front of an audience and speak in between songs – singing was easy, talking to people was not.

I found that drugs didn't help me when it came to going on stage, so I drank alcohol – just enough to allow me to be bubbly, but not enough to make me forget the words. I'd seen how band members taking different drugs could ruin things. One night, we had three guitarists on cannabis, while the drummer was on speed – he kept performing spontaneous drum solos, either in the middle of a song or at the end, drawing the usual hour-long set out to nearly two hours.

My relationship with Dick was a mess from day one. I found it hard to trust him, especially with all the loose girls chasing after him. As had happened with Kim, it wasn't long before my jealousy and aggressiveness drove him away. We couldn't live together, but we couldn't end it cleanly, so our relationship dragged on for a couple of months after he had left my home.

In October 1982, I moved from my flat to a two-bedroom house at the bottom of town. Dick moved to a nearby town called Lydney, where he shared a house with a fellow musician. One night, I risked my life to prove to Dick that I knew I was not being paranoid when I accused him of being with another woman eight miles away in Lydney while I was stuck in Cinderford, a town cut off by 5ft-high snow drifts.

As the clock struck midnight on New Year's Eve, I phoned Dick, as prearranged, to wish him a Happy New Year. He said he was on his own and that he had just left a neighbour's party to go home to take my call. Everything seemed fine until I heard the sound of a woman giggling in the background. I asked who was there. Dick sheepishly replied, 'No one, just me.'

I began accusing him of all sorts. I told him, 'Look, if you are with someone else just tell me so, and I'll consider us finished, but don't try to make out I'm mad or hearing things!'

Dick got angry with me at that, telling me it was all in my imagination and that I was being paranoid as usual. Then he slammed the phone down on me. I was so angry with him because I knew I had heard the giggling. It wasn't my imagination playing tricks on me and I wasn't being paranoid! I would prove it! Selfishly, and obsessed with the idea of catching Dick in the act of betrayal, I dragged little Kelly out of bed, dressed her, wrapped both her and myself up warm and carried her from my home at the bottom of town to my mum's.

It was all uphill and the snow was now approaching 2ft deep, it would normally take about fifteen minutes to get to my mum's, but in the snow it had taken me forty minutes. Mum was really angry with me for being out in the snow with Kelly at that time of night and told me I was a mad, selfish bitch. She was right, of course, but at that time all I wanted was to get to Dick's and prove to him and myself that I was right by catching him at it with another woman.

The snow had completely cut Cinderford off from the outside world, but I struggled with great effort to get through it. I was fuelled by my fuming determination that I would catch the cheating scoundrel at it!

I scaled and clambered over the snowdrifts as I made my slow and treacherous journey out of Cinderford. The snow was so deep that I had to use the tops of fences as a guide to where the road was. I laboured on through the whiteout and managed to trudge to the main road the A48, which was just passable for traffic. When I reached the main road it was 1.30am. I saw just one vehicle, a Land rover. I flagged it down and a bewildered couple returning home from a family party gave me a lift to Lydney.

I arrived just in time to set eyes on Dick, arm-in-arm with a vivacious girl called Polly, leaving his house. They were laughing together. Boy, was he surprised to see me!

I shouted at Dick, 'So this is my imaginary giggling female is it?'

They were both completely dumbfounded to see me. I finished with him on sight ... and then, unable to get back to Cinderford, I got snowed in with him for the next two days! In that time I had the chance to calm down. We talked and both decided it had been over for weeks really and that we would be better off as friends. After simmering down, I felt I deserved what I got for stealing him from another girl in the first place.

After Dick I went out with Nigel, a man some nine years my junior, for two years. That was a very tempestuous relationship. We were so alike that we clashed; it had to end before one of us killed the other. But we remained good friends. Then, after that, I had an eight-month relationship with another Dave, one of the sweetest men I know, but my insecurities got the better of me and the added stress of his disapproving mother soon put an end to things.

13

MY LOVEABLE ROGUE

IN 1985, I started hanging around with the local motorcycle club members. These bikers were classed as the bad boys of the Forest; they were known then as the Desperados and eventually became known as the Outlaws. They wore their 'patches' with pride and worked hard to earn them. Not just anyone could become a Desperado. First, you had to prove your loyalty to the other gang members; then you had to be willing to die for your bro (brother) if the need be.

I had first got to know most of them as customers when I was working at the Lion in 1981. I'd known their leader, Edge, since I was at school – at first by reputation, then when I was nineteen years old I got to know him personally by literally bumping into him at a disco. As I was leaving the bar, he turned around suddenly and accidentally knocked my drink out of my hand.

Before looking up, I fumed, 'Whoever did that can bloody well buy me another drink, that was my last pound!'

I nearly died on the spot when this tall, muscular man in leathers and long black hair said, 'OK, keep your pants on.' It was Edge! I'd spoken to him in a way that he was not accustomed to. Had I been a man, he would have punched me out for less.

I was pleasantly surprised by his gentle manner – not at all what I would have expected of him going by his reputation. He bought me a drink and returned to his group of friends, winking at me now and then from across the room.

After that, I didn't cross paths with Edge very often but the times that I did he was always nice to me. When he started drinking regularly at the Lion, I got to know him and the biker club quite well. I had been out with a couple of them and I enjoyed going around with them, except when they got into fights. They loved their bikes and their lifestyle, in that order, and they didn't take any messing from anyone.

In the summer months, they would invite other clubs down to the Forest and put on parties in the woods, and the local bands would play for them. I had some of my best times in their company and I fell in love with one of them.

Gary Tawse had just moved down from Manchester to join the Desperados. His first words to me were, 'Do you wanna sheep?' He and his mate, Johnny, had hit one of the free-roaming sheep from the Forest and put it in the boot of their car.

Even though he was only 23 years old, he looked older and craggy with his goatee beard and long, dark, lank hair hanging over his face. All I could see of him was his wide mouth, which looked even wider when he grinned. His clothes were dirty, he was definitely not what I was looking for in a man, but during our first conversation he asked me out and he told me he would never hurt me if I were his girlfriend.

We started out seeing each other as mates. Later, he moved in with me, as he had no real place to live. That first evening, he had a bath while I washed all his clothes. When he came back in the lounge he looked completely different. I was quite taken aback by how well he had scrubbed up. His greasy dark hair was in fact a light brown, he had combed it back off his clean face and, for the first time, I could see his blue eyes; he looked lovely. He reminded me of pictures of Jesus, and I felt instantly attracted to him. We had to share my bed while he stayed with me, but I would just give him a kiss good night, then turn away from him to sleep.

One day, Gary said, 'What's wrong with me, Caroline, why don't you want me?' He looked so hurt and vulnerable. I told him the truth: I liked him too much and I was scared of starting anything up with him because all my relationships had been ruined by my jealousy.

I let my 'happy face' mask drop that night and we talked, and I cried as I told him how I had mistreated all my ex-boyfriends and what a cold-hearted bitch I had been. Gary wasn't worried about any of it – he told me that he loved me and would do anything to stay with me. 'Even get a job!' he chuckled.

That night, we became lovers. We were happy even though – perhaps unsurprisingly – I sometimes got jealous of him talking to other girls. If he saw me looking moody, he would hold me in a gentle bear hug and tell me that he would never do anything to hurt me and that he would never leave me. When I asked him why he put up with me, he would give me one of his silly smiles and say, 'Because I love you, you silly cow.'

A month after we had become lovers, Gary asked me to marry him and I said, 'Yes.' We decided we would just go to the Register Office, get wed and go home with a bottle of Southern Comfort and a Chinese take-away, as we couldn't afford anything more. When we told my sister, Sue, she offered to pay for the wedding licence, so we planned to get married in the December of 1985.

On 25 October 1985, on the eve of my thirtieth birthday, we had had such a lovely day together. Gary usually looked rough in the mornings, but on that particular morning he looked quite handsome.

After taking Kelly to school, I climbed back into bed with Gary and during the course of that day we made passionate love three times. This wasn't the norm; it was as if it had some deep spiritual meaning that was to be revealed in what was to happen later that night.

We were messing around and laughing a lot. The only slight tiff we had was about me accidentally taping Bob Dylan's 'Knockin' On Heaven's Door' from the radio on to an AC/DC tape Gary had off my mate Sally. He told me that he had an album with that song on at his mate Johnny's and would give it to me.

We were intending to spend an hour or two with Sue that day, as she was due to have a baby and we were on standby in case she went in. I was going to look after her three-year-old daughter Jemma, but we phoned and cancelled and spent the whole day cuddling.

Later on, my good friend Dave Reed called in with some wine for me, then my brother Rick did the same. Both commented on our hyper-happy mood, asking if they could have some of what we were on. I told them, 'It isn't any drugs … it's love!'

As it was a Friday, Gary had arranged to go to Johnny's for tea and then on to the club meeting, which was eight miles away in Monmouth. Friday was always a late night; the whole bikers' club would usually go to a nightclub and then back to Jacky and Mark's house for a party.

If I wasn't with him, Gary would go to the nightclub before coming home to me. I would go on to bed and, hours later, I would hear Gary's run-down Suzuki pull up outside. The Suzuki was in such a shoddy condition that I often wondered how it kept going. It seemed to be held together with bits of wire and insulation tape.

I had suffered, and enjoyed, enough of all the weekends out and the constant boozing and drug taking, so I was happy to stay in on a Friday and relax. On this particular Friday, we had enjoyed each other's company so much that neither of us really wanted it to end, but club business was important so, reluctantly, he had to go.

Gary said, 'I'll only take three quid with me. That way I'll have an excuse to come home early and see your birthday in with you.'

He really didn't want to go. He kept putting his foot inside the front door so I couldn't shut it and kept grabbing a hold of me and saying, 'I don't want to go, let me stay with you.'

I told him, 'Sally's coming round to see my birthday in with me, I'll see you later.'

Gary said, 'OK, I'm going, but don't start drinking till I get back. I want to see your birthday in with you too.'

While we were still both giggling, I shut the door on him and he rode off, grinning his silly grin and waving.

My mate Sally Peacey came round later that evening with a Chinese take-away and a bottle of wine. Kelly was tucked up in bed, fast asleep. I was laughing as I recalled my day for Sally. She was glad to see me so happy. We were both in high spirits by the time Gary was due home.

At midnight, we opened our third bottle of wine, expecting Gary to arrive shortly. By 12.30am, he still wasn't back so we started drinking it.

Minutes later, we heard a motorbike pull up and then a knock on the door. I was still laughing as I opened the door, but it wasn't Gary, it was his mate Dylan Owens. He was usually a bit of a joker, but he looked deadly serious and humourless as he took me into the kitchen and told me, 'I'm sorry, Caroline, but there has been an accident. Gary's dead.'

Before I could react, I heard another bike pull up and scowled at Dylan for telling sick jokes. I went to the door expecting to see Gary, but it was Rob, another club member. He just looked at me with pity in his eyes and pain etched into his face as he said, 'You've heard then?'

I felt my knees trembling and my heart lurch as they went on to tell me the dreadful thing that had happened. Gary had sneaked away from the rest of the club so he could get home by midnight to see my birthday in with me. Some other bikers had found his bike lying in the road Gary had been thrown off. They found him some yards away from his bike, but he was dead. The helmet he had worn, which had no padding, had not protected him. He had died instantly from serious head injuries. He had wanted to be with me, and it had cost him his life.

I spent my birthday identifying Gary's body. Right up until the time I got to see him lying there in a small white room at Gloucester Royal Hospital's A&E department, I was still hoping it had all been a big mistake and that it wouldn't be my lovable rogue – but it was. As I got closer to his cold, wet body, I was still expecting him to suddenly jump up and say, 'Boo! Fooled ya!' But he didn't.

A crack ran from the front of his hairline and over the back of his head. It was a shocking sight that would normally have made me throw up, even if it had only been in a film on the TV, but I found no repulsion in what I saw. All I saw was the man I loved. I stroked his wet hair back from his face and kissed his cold cheek and told him what a fool he was for sneaking off, and that I loved him and would love him for the rest of my life.

When Sally and I got back home, she sat in my bedroom with me. The first thing I noticed was that the Jesus figure had fallen off the crucifix that Gary had given me. The crucifix he had taken from a gay guy whom he had hung out of a sixteenth-floor window, for a laugh, on his last night out in Birmingham with another club, the Cycle Tramps. I had been angry about what he had done and he promised me that he wouldn't do anything stupid like that again.

Later that morning, Dylan picked me up and we rode up to Manchester to break the news to Gary's parents and sisters. I had only met them once, two weeks earlier when Gary, who had been the black sheep of the family, had decided it was time to see them. He wanted to show them that he was settled down with a 'nice girl', someone his mum could approve of, not like the last girl he had taken home – a 'foul-mouthed punkette'.

I had got on well with his family during that overnight stay, and Gary's mum was well impressed with the fact that I had talked Gary into having his hair cut shorter and styled.

'He must really care for you to have had his hair cut,' she said with a smile on her face and added, 'I've tried bribing him with money just to clean himself up and get his hair trimmed, and now here he is, just as I imagined he would look. Thank you, you must be good for him.'

She went on to tell me how she despaired of him and that her worst fear was that he would end up being killed on his bike or in prison. And as I waited to tell her that her worst fear had just come true, I cried. Losing Gary had broken my heart. I vowed I would never let myself fall in love again. I really was a jinx. Tragedy on an unremitting scale had invaded my life.

The following week, Gary was buried at Leigh, in Manchester. There were hundreds of bikers from all the different MC (motorcycle) clubs and his old mates from Manchester way were at his funeral. All were on bikes and, in defiance of the law, helmets were off in a show of respect for Gary.

The Desperados carried Gary's coffin into the church. I remember looking at them all – they looked so out of place, so uncomfortable with their surroundings, all fidgety, but they did it for Gary and his family. I was sat there cursing God for taking my man.

I had been to say my goodbyes to Gary in the Chapel of

Rest; his body lay there wrapped in a pretty white satin shroud. His hair was combed wrong; he had make up on. I touched his bruised hand, which felt cold and waxy. He looked like a mannequin, a shell of my Gary. His body was there but his spirit had left his body. I hoped he was in a different world, a better world, but I had my doubts.

The Desperados placed Gary's patches on top of his coffin, as they lowered it into the ground and filled the grave up with soil. This responsibility was not left to the gravediggers – it had to be done with reverence, showing Gary the respect that he deserved, the respect that came from the brothers of his club.

After the funeral, in the club's tradition, there was a big send-off party in his honour. Although I was amongst many friends, I had never felt so alone as I did that night. On the card I attached to the heart-shaped wreath I wrote:

You were everything I wasn't looking for,
But you were all I ever needed.
There is no Beauty without my Beast.

14

'MARJORIE PROOPS' AND 'CLAIRE RAYNER'

SOME STRANGE THINGS happened to me during the days following Gary's funeral. The first happened when we were all at a friend's large country house the day after the funeral. Jackie and Mark Wallman were two good friends of the Desperados and had held many all-night parties at their house for the lads. We had gone back there for the night to chill out and get ourselves together.

Mark was an author and he had spent many months living amongst the Afghan rebels in the eighties, during the war between Russia and Afghanistan. He had written a book about his experiences and was in between books when I met him. The Wallmans had also spent a lot of time living in India and were very spiritual people.

I asked Jackie where she thought Gary was, and whether she believed that we lived on in another universe somewhere. 'Yes,' she said, she believed we did.

I said to her, 'I've got to see a vicar, I need to talk to one, someone of any religious denomination. I can't sleep not knowing where he is.'

It was a sunny, though cold, Sunday morning. I told my lift that I would walk on into Monmouth and meet them in the pub. I just wanted to be on my own, alone with nothing but my thoughts for company. Carrying my motorcycle helmet, I walked through the narrow country lanes thinking of Gary. Tears were rolling down my face as I cried in silence. I was wrapped up in my own lonely little world.

Suddenly, I was brought back to reality when a little old man who was latching open the gates to his drive said, 'Are you all right, my dear?' The man had a real look of concern on his face. I felt embarrassed, as I realised someone, a stranger, had seen me crying. Where had my 'happy face' gone?

I quickly pulled myself together, said, 'I'm fine,' tried to smile a smile and walked past him.

He called after me, 'Where are you going? Do you need a lift?'

I told him I was walking into Monmouth to meet friends and he said, 'Well, if you wait a second, my friend and I can give you a lift. We're passing through Monmouth.'

He seemed so nice and caring that I accepted his offer and waited by the gate for him to get the car out of the drive. I was so shocked when I got into the car and saw that he and his friend were both wearing what are commonly known as dog collars … they were both vicars! I was so shocked that, even though I'd really wanted to see a vicar, I couldn't bring myself to ask all the questions that seemed so urgent before. I was stunned into silence.

I took this to be a sign that maybe, after all, there was a God and that He had, indeed, answered my questions, or rather my need, by not only getting me one vicar but two! Even stranger to my mind was the fact that the two vicars were on their way to give a service in the village of Staunton, between Monmouth and Cinderford. Staunton was where Gary had crashed his bike and died on that cold and wet October evening.

I was glad to get home, to get back to our room and cuddle up to Gary's old overcoat. I could still smell him on his coat and it comforted me. This was one of those times when I would have most probably tried to kill myself if it wasn't for the fact that I had a daughter who needed me, someone who loved me unconditionally – just like Gary had. I felt so worried about Gary. I was so scared, he was in some kind of hell because of all the bad things he had done in his lifetime, and I missed him terribly.

During that week, I had visitors from all different religions calling on me. The vicar from my local church of St Stephen's knew of Gary's death, and came to offer me support and a prayer for Gary. The Jehovah's Witnesses and the Mormons called in, unaware that I needed them; they were simply carrying out the usual routine of knocking on doors. Normally, I would make some polite excuse and send them on their way, but this time I was pleased to welcome them in so I could cross-examine them to find out what they thought had become of Gary – or at least his soul, his spirit. They were all really kind and considerate and they tried to put my mind at rest, but I was still fretting. I couldn't sleep at night, I was angry and exhausted and, I'm ashamed to say, I took it out on my loved ones, including my five-year-old daughter, Kelly.

The only person I could talk to was my good friend and agony aunt, Dave Reed. Dave was my comfort – he didn't mind my ranting, raving and cursing. I felt bitter and resentful, and wished it had been someone else who had died, not my Gary. I had been cheated out of happiness.

That night, while we were talking about Gary, the curtains suddenly bellowed out into the room, as if a gust of wind had caught them. I jumped up to close the window but found it was already shut tight.

'What could have caused that to happen?' I asked Dave.

'I expect that's Gary trying to let you know he's still around, listening to you,' Dave replied in a laid-back way.

We went on to discuss our thoughts on life after death and after talking for a while we agreed that whichever of us died first should come back and let the other know what it's like. Just like when the escapologist Houdini had told his wife a password that he would reveal to her again after he was dead, we too needed some sort of codeword that we could use to confirm that contact had been made with whichever one of us was dead. We decided that we would use the agony aunt names that we called each other as our passwords: Dave was 'Marjorie Proops' and I was 'Claire Rayner'.

The rest of that week, many astonishing and bizarre happenings occurred. I lay in bed one night, a few days after the funeral, feeling very down and lonely. I lay there with my eyes closed, although I was still awake. Suddenly, I felt I wasn't alone; I had the feeling that there was someone else in the dark with me. At first, I was scared – too scared to open my eyes. Then I felt someone sit on the edge of my bed; I felt the weight and the indentation, it was real.

I froze with fear and held my breath. Then I felt someone kiss me on my cheek. It felt so real, I knew then that it was Gary. I opened my eyes but could see nothing so I closed them again. Then I felt him get into bed with me and was overwhelmed with a feeling of peace that washed over me. I drifted off to sleep but was woken some time later by a brilliant bright light shining on my bedroom wall, almost like an old-fashioned film projector.

I saw images of a winding road; it was night time. I saw a headlight coming towards me, then I was behind it and I saw the taillight. I took it to be Gary's motorbike. Again, I was in front of it and, as it approached me on a straight stretch of road, the light went out and it was gone. I was unquestionably awake when I saw all of this because I used the bathroom straight afterwards. I went back to bed and fell asleep.

The next night I had a very vivid dream – well, I think it was a dream. Gary came for me and took me for a walk down a tree-lined lane. The branches of the trees hung like silk lace, forming an inviting archway. The shafts of sunlight were pouring through the leaves, making dancing patterns on the ground. We were strolling hand in hand. I looked up at Gary and said, 'You've changed, you look different.'

Then I realised: the goatee beard had gone. I'd never seen him without his beard before; he looked strange. I felt really happy and contented and tried to kiss him, but he gently held me away from him and said, 'We don't do that here,' then added, 'I've brought you here to show you that I'm all right. You mustn't keep willing me to come back to you. I went before my time, but I'm happy now and you can stop worrying about me and get on with your life. I will always love you and I will always be there when you need me, but you must let me go.'

With that said, he hugged me and smiled and I was back in my bed. The next day, I felt much happier and decided that Gary was somewhere wonderful and all that my pining was doing was making it harder for him to settle down in his new life.

Then something happened. I wasn't even thinking about Gary at the time. I had been struggling to get my figures right in readiness to send my catalogue payment in for my clothes. I'd been at it for an hour or more and it didn't tally up right.

I was £22 short and worrying that I would end up out of pocket if I had to put the money in myself. Money was short and Christmas was only weeks away. I was deeply engrossed in my calculations when I heard a knock at the door.

As I made my way to the front door, I looked up at the clock – it was 11.15pm. I was feeling irritated that someone would call at the house at that time of night and I was ready to curse whoever it was. I opened the door, expecting to see some sort of wretched face, but there was no one there! Yet I felt a presence! This presence I knew to be Gary. If anyone had seen me they would have said I was mad, but I said, 'Come on in, I've missed you.'

I felt him follow me into the living room. It was then that I realised that it was exactly four weeks to the day, and time, that Gary had been killed. I sat back down on the floor and got on with my mathematical problem, telling Gary that I couldn't work out why the cash I had collected in didn't tally with the paperwork.

Then, suddenly, it came to me: one of my customers had given me her money, but I'd left it on her kitchen table. It was only a thought that came into my head, but I think it was Gary that put it there. When my problem was solved, I could no longer feel Gary's presence. It was as if he just wanted to help me so I could stop worrying and go to bed.

15

A TRAUMATIC FLASHBACK

IN AUGUST 1987, I married Gary's best friend, Dylan Owens.
Dylan had always had a soft spot for me, even though it had
been Gary that had got me. When I lost Gary, Dylan was there
for me. I had agreed before Gary's death that Dylan could move
in with us when the snow came, as there was no way he could
get to work on his bike from the cottage he was renting out in
the countryside at Tintern. When winter came, Dylan moved
into Kelly's room and she moved in with me.

Having a man about the house again was nice. I enjoyed
Dylan's company. We would sit and talk about all the things
he and Gary got up to when they lived in Runcorn,
Cheshire, on the edge of Liverpool and Manchester. They
were bad guys with good hearts and would do anything for
money and a laugh.

One night, I invited a male friend, Phil Green, back to the

house for supper. We were sitting in the kitchen eating when Dylan suddenly burst in and, for no reason, attacked Phil in an uncontrolled rage. I dragged Dylan off Phil, told him to apologise and then asked him to leave.

Later, when things had calmed down, I asked Dylan why he had done it. He said he suddenly felt wildly jealous; he hadn't realised how much I meant to him until he saw me with someone else and this had pushed him into a frenzied abandonment. That was how Dylan and I came to be a couple.

After a year, we had a big fall-out and split up. Dylan ended up staying at my sister Angela's as her lodger. We hadn't seen each other for a month or so when Dylan asked me if I would go out for a drink with him, as he wanted to talk. We were sat in a pub talking when Edge, the leader of the Desperados, and some of the boys came in. I could tell from the look that Edge gave me that he was not pleased to see me.

I went to the toilets. Edge was waiting for me as I came out.

He asked me, 'What are you up to, messing Dyl around?'

I replied, 'It's none of your business,' and walked straight past him focussing on the door to the bar. I didn't want to make eye contact with Edge, I didn't want to get caught in the 'Edge glare' like a rabbit caught in the headlights.

Edge roared at me, as I defiantly walked passed him, 'You don't mess with Dyl, right! Sort things out, now!'

I shoved my nose up in the air and strutted away, looking a lot cockier than I really felt.

That was one of the few times Edge and me nearly came to blows. I thank God he never did connect his fist to my face. I'd seen him do it before, to men, and the results were pretty horrific.

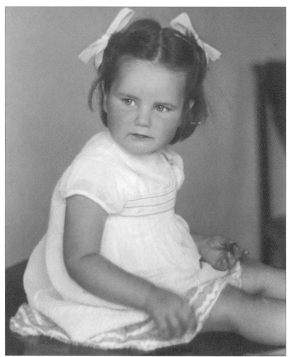

Top: My brother Phillip aged 7, Mum and me, aged 5. A rare day at the beach.

Left: Me aged 18 months.

Sporting my 'Dave-from-Slade' haircut (*above*) aged 16 in 1972, a few months before the Wests employed me and with my friend Julie (*right*).

The chilling portrait of Fred and Rose that went around the world at the time of their arrest.

In the aftermath of my time with the Wests, I tried to keep my 'happy face' on.

Posing for the camera aged 19 in 1974 (*top left*) and in Western Super-Mare, just before I took an overdose in 1976 aged 20 (*top right*).

Bottom: In summer 1977 I became Miss Forest of Dean. Mum thought that winning the competition would give my confidence a boost.

My loveable rogue, Gary Tawse, killed on his way home to see my 30th birthday in. He is pictured here with a mate and with me, at a biker party, a month before he died.

Top: My friend Dave Reed (aka Marjorie Proops), who died aged 26.

Bottom: Out on Dylan's motorbike in the Forest of Dean.

Top: Berkley Mill where Fred West told his son, Steven West, that there were more remains of his victims. We got in to investigate by pretending we were interested in old buildings.

Bottom: Mum with Kelly in 1987. They were always very close.

Clockwise from top left: With Kelly aged 2, with Shani-Jade at 6 months, with Liam at 5 months and Shannon at 10 weeks.

I didn't get back with Dylan immediately – that happened after I had yet another fall-out with some club members. The Desperados had merged with the Cycle Tramps and some other MC clubs, and had become a much larger club under the Cycle Tramps name. This seemed to go the heads of some of the local club members. One night, I was at a funeral party; it was the first time I'd been in the club's company since Edge and I had our fall out in the pub. Some of the lads started getting out of hand. One man, Rob, was picking fights with some of the friends of the deceased. I've always been one to protect others; especially the underdog, and I could no longer bear to watch, so I started pulling Rob away from the lad.

Rob, not seeing who it was that had a hold of him from behind, accidentally elbowed me in the eye. Dylan saw it happen, grabbed hold of Rob and threw a punch at him, a punch that would cost Dylan his full patches. The club relegated him back to being a lowly 'Prospect' (an apprentice), which meant he was back to square one with them.

Poor Dylan, he had become the gang's dog's body, the runaround, having to win back the respect of his bros; it wasn't an easy feat. I felt sorry for Dylan; he had lost it all because he cared about me. I had jinxed yet another one!

A week later, Dylan came to see me and asked if there was any chance that I'd have him back. He was miserable, he was having a hard time of it with the club, he felt he had nothing to stay for and was thinking of quitting his job, the club and the Forest of Dean to go back to a 'fish bowl' flat on a run-down estate in Runcorn. He was despondent and down in the dumps.

I knew if he threw the towel in he'd end up on drugs and

start dealing them to support his habit. Either that or he'd get thrown in jail for fighting. I knew quite a lot about how he existed there just by the things he had told me. I told him I'd think about it overnight.

By the next day I had made up my mind that I did love Dylan – maybe not as passionately as I should have, but I did love him – and that I would only have him back if we got married and moved away for a fresh start.

It was a Tuesday morning. I phoned up the local register office and asked about a 'Special Licence' and how soon I could get married. Then I phoned Dylan at work. When he answered the phone, I said, 'Do you still want me back?'

He said, 'Yeah!'

'OK, ask your boss, right now, if you can have next Monday off, 'cause you're getting married, it's all arranged. Is that OK with you?' I said, laughing as I put the phone down. Six days later we were wed.

Dylan gave up the bikers club, as he couldn't commit to both family and club. In November 1987, we moved to nearby Berry Hill and bought an ex-council house. I gave birth to my second daughter, Shani-Jade, on 24 August 1988, a year after our wedding.

I chose the name Shani (pronounced Shay-nee) when I heard it on the news. The name belonged to a suspected murder victim, who was found with her hands tied behind her back in a pond. The Shani who was dead had been on the way to drop some grass cuttings off after mowing her lawn, and was never seen alive again; no one was ever charged with her murder. This was a rather macabre way of choosing a name I know, but I thought it was a pretty name for my beautiful dark-haired baby and I would always remember that poor murdered girl not with sadness but with love. I felt so sorry for the victim's family; I know I couldn't cope if anything like that happened to my Shani.

I had been working full time since Shani-Jade was five months old. First, for a year at a chip shop, then a year at SmithKline-Beechams, in nearby Coleford, bottling up the soft drinks. While there, I dressed up as a voluptuous Bunny Girl and became a kissagram – for one night only – for a colleague, Ray, who was retiring.

Then I landed myself a very well-paid job at Rank Xerox in Mitcheldean. The photocopier company was the biggest employer in the Forest and offered the highest paid factory work in the county. I always thought that if I could have gone to work there when I was a teenager, I would have turned out a different girl, but I didn't get the job back in the seventies. I had to wait till I was in my thirties and tied down with responsibilities. How I would have saved and travelled if I had been on that money back then!

Dylan was working during the day and I was working a twilight shift. We hardly saw each other during the week, so it was little surprise that a strain began to develop in our relationship. I took solace by going out with my girlfriends on the weekends to nightclubs and I soon realised that I didn't want to be married any longer … a wedge of boredom had started our split. Dylan was a good husband and a devoted father, but there was no spark any more – well, not for me.

Meanwhile, Mum had found her long-lost brothers and

sister. Mum spoke to her sister Kath on the phone and arranged to meet up again for the first time in thirty years, but sadly Kath died unexpectedly in her sleep that very night and Mum eventually met her estranged brother, Ben, at Kath's funeral.

Kath's family contacted her other brother, Sid, who came over from Australia to meet us all. Mum and Sid got on well and Mum became quite possessive of him. When it was time for him to return home, he took my mum and my daughter, Kelly, back to Townsville, in Australia, with him for six months – the happiest six months of my dear mum's life. She thought the world of her newly acquainted brother and every minute they spent together was precious to her.

I had missed Kelly and worried about her while she was so far away from me. Kelly would phone me every week, and even though she was enjoying herself and had made friends at school, she always started to cry at the end of the calls, which would start me off too.

On the day they returned, Dylan and I went to meet them at Heathrow Airport. I felt a lump in my throat when I saw Mum and Sid walking towards me, and rushed forward to give them a hug and a kiss.

I looked around for Kelly, but I couldn't see her. Then, suddenly, I spotted a big girl racing towards me; it took a second to recognise her as Kelly. While Kelly was gone, she had grown so much; she was as tall as me and had put on a lot of weight. After running up to me, she hugged me so tight I could hardly breathe. 'I missed you, Mum,' she said, laughing and crying at the same time.

I could hardly believe she was the same little girl I had waved goodbye to some six months earlier. I held her for a second but found, to my horror, that out of nowhere Rose West's face had suddenly sprang to mind. Kelly had held on too tightly and for too long. I panicked and went into a different dimension; I was rankled and I pushed her away. Much to my horror, and the astonishment of Sid, Mum and Dylan, I found myself shouting, 'Get off me!'

Instantly, I saw the hurt that come over Kelly's chubby little face and I knew there was nothing I could do to comfort her. She had been away from me all that time and I had rejected her on her return. My reaction had been simply a reflex, but that second's thoughtlessness was to be the start of years of hurt for Kelly. I wanted to tell Kelly why I had responded in that way, but how could I tell my ten-year-old daughter that when she hugged me too tight it repulsed me and brought back memories of a female rapist? Worryingly, I began to find that I couldn't show her physical affection any more, and I feared it would be the same with Shani-Jade as she got older and bigger.

This experience at the airport had shaken me up, but I knew that there were other aspects of my life that needed addressing too. I decided to get a divorce, as I felt trapped and ensnared in a marriage with a man I couldn't love the way he deserved. It wasn't an easy decision to make. I went to marriage guidance for counselling, as I felt so guilty knowing how much it would hurt Dylan. I prepared him for the separation by telling him in the August that I would be leaving after Christmas. I knew he would get over losing me, but losing Shani-Jade would really hurt him.

16

AMONGST THE MADDING CROWD

1992

ON NEW YEAR'S DAY 1992, I took three-year-old Shani-Jade and Kelly, who was just turning twelve, and moved back to Cinderford. To start with, we stayed at my brother Rob's as he was on his own after his wife had run off with her boss. After three months, Rob got himself fixed up with a girlfriend, so I needed somewhere else to live.

Our next home was a run-down terraced cottage that a friend rented out to us as a stop-gap. The place was in a dilapidated condition and was a dangerous environment for the children. And for me: one night I fell down the steep narrow staircase. I was left with bruising that ran all down one side of my head and body.

The fall cost me time off work, which wasn't a problem as it meant I could look after the children. A regular babysitter was proving hard to find. Most of the time, the girls had to stay at my mum's and sleep the night there – either that or be dragged out at midnight back home with me. I asked the Department of Health & Social Security for some help, but I earned £5 a week too much to claim any money, so I couldn't afford a babysitter. In the end, I gave up and decided to use what savings I had as a deposit on renting a nicer, safer house.

In the June, we moved into 2 Albion Place, a two-bedroom house at the bottom of Cinderford High Street. I gave up my job at Rank Xerox to look after the children and went on to state benefits. I was happy living on my own and had no intentions of settling down again.

Every weekend, Dylan had Shani-Jade and Kelly went to stay with my mum. I took advantage of this free time by going out to the local pubs and, as a consequence, I got back into singing, though this time only for karaoke, not as part of a band.

Nicky Bower, a friend of mine from my days at Hilldene, ran the disco karaoke and encouraged me to get up and sing. At first I was petrified but, once I got a positive response from the crowd, I really enjoyed myself. My sister Sue and I would do a duet, a suggestive version of the Audrey Hepburn song 'I Could Have Danced All Night'; the crowd loved it.

Some nights, it was more like the Caroline and Sue Show, as we tended to hog the stage. They were good times; we had a good crowd of friends who knew how to enjoy themselves. I was enjoying my freedom; I had made up my mind that I was happier without a man to worry about or run around after. I liked to see a man when I felt like it – nothing heavy, no ties, just fun.

1993

I met nineteen-year-old Ian Roberts at a karaoke competition in March 1993; at 38 years old I was old enough to be his mum! But what started out as a bit of fun, a short fling, ended up with me becoming pregnant on our second date due to a condom coming off, and all hell broke loose.

Ian's parents, who were only a couple of years older than me, were in uproar when they found out that their youngest of two sons was not only seeing a single mum with two children who had a bit of reputation, but was also to become a father to our child – and they still harboured hopes of disputing the paternity.

I had given Ian the chance to leave me. I had even suggested we say the baby was that of an ex-boyfriend who didn't live around our area. But Ian did the honourable thing and said that he wanted to help bring his child up and be a father to it, so we decided to keep seeing each other.

This was one of the worst years of my life. Ian, only being a lad, was always telling me little lies and being deceitful. He lied to me, he lied to his parents, he lied to keep the peace and to keep everyone happy. After only four months, I wanted to bring an end to our relationship, but he got extremely upset and promised there would be no more deceit, so I gave in to him, even though we had to keep the affair a secret because of his family.

When Ian got home from work, he would come to see me and then he'd drive back home to his parents at the same time each evening for his tea, so his parents didn't suspect a thing. Ian would have to hide the work van that he used around the back of the house so no one could see it.

We had friends who ran the Swan pub, and that was the only place we could go out to where we could feel accepted as a couple. On the occasions his brother and his rugby-playing mates came in, Ian would have to move away from me or suffer verbal abuse from his brother and his brother's mates. Some of them would tell him he shouldn't be tying himself down to an old tart like me. I found it all very hurtful and humiliating but said nothing.

Because of my age, I opted for an amniocentesis test to be carried out when I was nineteen weeks' pregnant. (This is a procedure whereby a hollow needle is inserted into the uterus and fluid is taken out so as to check the foetus for abnormalities.) I had to wait three weeks for the results. It was worrying time for us both because, although I knew I couldn't cope with a Downs Syndrome child, I knew I couldn't go through with an abortion. But I still felt I had to know.

While I was at home worrying, Ian was off holidaying to Crete, having fun in the sun. The holiday, with a group of friends from Cinderford Rugby Club, had been booked some time previously. Everyday, sometimes twice a day, he would phone me, saying he was missing me and wanted to come home – and this was only in the first week. I decided I would go away for the second week that he was away.

I got a late booking to Corfu with my friend Sally and two days later I, too, was lying on a beach. The location was very quiet, the locals still carried firewood around on a donkey, and a shepherdess, bent over double with age, still took her goats to graze every morning and collected them each evening, herding them across the beach to the hills. Corfu was a lovely quiet place; the sunshine and peace was heaven for me.

I arrived back at my house from holiday at 7.00am – exactly the same time Ian arrived back from his holiday. We were both tanned and both happy to be together once more. I was looking forward to seeing my girls again, as I had missed them so much. They had been staying with my mum. I intended to sleep till noon and saunter over and pick them up, as both Ian and I were tired. We'd been up most of the night waiting to fly home from our respective holidays and we just wanted to go to bed. As we entered the front door, I saw a hand-delivered envelope, which I picked up.

The note was from the midwife telling me to phone the hospital immediately as there was a problem with the test results. The baby had a chromosome disorder and the paediatrician needed to talk to us as soon as possible. I just knew it: my bad luck syndrome had been lurking around just waiting to strike me down again, but this time it was too much to bear.

As we drove to the hospital, a half-hour journey to Gloucester, I felt sure I would be staying in to have an abortion. Ian had said he didn't want us to have the baby if it was badly deformed or handicapped. I could see he was upset too, though he was quiet.

I was ranting and shouting and blaming an LSD tab I'd taken before I'd known I was pregnant. It was a one-off experience, I had just wanted to try it, and other friends had used the drug and said it was mind-bending, literally. I'd smoked dope and taken speed before, but never any hallucinogenic types of drugs – I was too scared! I was frightened some bad memories would flashback to haunt me – God knows, I had enough of them – but they didn't. No demons, no monsters, and no Fred and Rose

West. I had a good trip, which had lasted all night. I never meant to hurt anyone else by taking it but now I was thinking, what if I had caused something to be wrong with my baby? I felt so angry and guilty; I wanted to punch someone or something. Most of all, I wanted to punch myself hard in the head for being such a stupid, selfish bitch.

When we got to the hospital, I went into the antenatal waiting room to let them know I had arrived, but immediately I felt I had to go back outside again. I just couldn't face all the other pregnant women there, knowing they would get to hold their babies and watch them grow while I was about to force mine, prematurely, from my body and it would be taken away from me for good.

Within ten minutes, we were led into a small office where a secretary kindly asked us if we wanted a cup of tea.

I couldn't stop crying. 'It's unfair, it's so unfair!'

Ian held my hand, trying to comfort me, but he was shaking with emotion too. Two doctors came in and sat facing us; the expressions on their faces were serious. They told us that the child I was carrying had Turner's Syndrome. They went on to describe all the defects and problems that our child might have. At first, we were horror-struck. Then one of the doctors went on to tell us that the baby was a little girl and that if she did survive, she would be very small and would have to have growth hormones to help her grow till she reached a satisfactory height. He added that she would not be able to have children, as her ovaries wouldn't work and could turn cancerous – they would have to be removed.

Those last two details stirred up memories of a conversation

I had had with my sister, Sue, who had discovered that her daughter Jemma had a chromosome disorder. I mentioned Jemma to the doctors and they said that Jemma had Turner's Syndrome too. They were both surprised that two sisters could both have Turner's Syndrome girls – there's a million-to-one chance of it occurring twice in the same family. Armed with that knowledge, and knowing what a lovely little girl eleven-year-old Jemma was, I decided I would keep my baby as long as her heart was OK. I didn't want to bring her into this world if it meant her having lots of painful surgery. We went to Bristol Children's Hospital and had the baby's heart scanned while she was in my womb. The doctor said he could see no problem with her heart. I was so happy that I cried with relief and I hugged Sue, who had driven me to the hospital.

We talked all the way home about Turner's and then got on to the subject of names. I decided to name my baby Shannon Lacey, still keeping that link with Ireland and my biological father.

During the pregnancy I was scanned regularly to check that Shannon was still growing. She was small but not too small. All through that time I had hassle from Ian's family to deal with. They were demanding blood tests to prove that the baby was his child. Ian's brother had been talking in the hairdressers, telling the staff there that the baby was not Ian's and that I had got pregnant on purpose to trap myself a young man. The rumour quickly spread and soon got back to me.

Yet again, I was humiliated at a time that should have been a joy. Other people marred my joy with their scurrilous accusations and snide remarks. Their brains were going in reverse and their mouths were going forwards.

My close friends told me to ignore it, but it was hard. In the past I was able to see my good friend Dave Reed, my very own Majorie Proops, when I had problems, but he had moved away from the Forest to Gloucester after he had come out of the closet, as they say, in 1985. The narrow-minded small-town folk of the Forest had made it hard for Dave to be himself, so he had moved into the city, where he had many gay friends. In between 1985 and 1992, life had been difficult for Dave. Being open about his sexual preference had caused him some problems, problems that even I couldn't help him sort out. By 1987, he had become ill and was diagnosed as being a manic depressive. For a couple of years, Dave was in and out of Coney Hill Mental Hospital … the hospital I always dreaded having to visit! Coney Hill was the hospital that my attacker in Gloucester Park came from. In my mind, the attacker was still there. Every old man I saw in that place, on the few occasions I could bring myself to actually go there, was to me a replica of my attacker.

When I saw Dave at the hospital, I would be so sad to see him all doped up on medication. My wild, flamboyant Dave, the party animal, was reduced to being a zombie. Seeing Dave taking tiny shuffling footsteps, usually around in circles, with his mouth opening and closing like a goldfish, made me squirm with shock. The once-handsome face, a shadow of its former self, was now bloated from the extra weight he had gained while shuffling along.

Dave had done well after moving to the city. He was always one to get people motivated and doing something. It wasn't long before he and some friends were busy getting a Survivors' Group set up. The group was for people who were suffering with depression, and offered help and support to them. Dave was busy organising his group and had not been in touch with me for some time. One evening, I suddenly thought of him and said to Ian, 'I haven't spoken to Dave for months, do you think it's too late to phone him now?'

It was ten o'clock. I went to pick up the phone to call him and, as I did, it rang. On the other end of the line was Dave! He said he had been thinking of me and decided to phone me; we both laughed when I told him, 'We must be telepathic, like twins are supposed to be.' We had a chat and Dave was very positive about my problems, telling me that Ian's parents would come around in the end, and that the baby would be fine and beautiful like her mother.

I told Dave that Shani-Jade was behaving strangely. She was mutilating her dolls and blaming Ian and Kelly for it and she was always being cheeky to Ian and downright horrible to me. Dave didn't think I should worry about her too much, and had a sensible explanation for her behaviour: 'She's just missing her dad, that's all, and she feels threatened by the new baby and Ian taking over as the dad in the house.' He reminded me that I had behaved the same when I was around Shani-Jade's age, when Mum married Alf and Sue was on the way. He was right – as usual. Dave knew me better than anyone else, my good points and my bad points, and he still loved me. He was a true friend.

On 17 November 1993, I had an appointment at Gloucester Hospital and told Dave I would call in to see him before I went for the scan. I was excited when I arrived at his flat because I wanted to ask him to be at the birth, as Ian might be away. I was going to invite him to come with me for the scan that day; I knew he would want to.

I got to his flat on time and knocked on the door, but there was no answer. It wasn't like Dave to let me down. I thought that maybe he had been called away urgently, but he would have left a note on his door in that case. I knocked, waited ten minutes and then left with a funny feeling in my gut that something wasn't quite right.

Two days later, Dave's mum phoned to tell me that Dave had been found dead in his bedroom. He had been dead for days. A deliberate overdose of his medication was responsible for Dave's death.

I was shattered. I loved Dave and would miss him forever; he was the only one I could be myself with, my true friend. At the crematorium, they played the Shirley Bassey song 'Hey Big Spender', which was a favourite of Dave's. I recalled how he would prance about in my bedroom while dressed in drag ready to go to a charity drag party, and chuckled to myself. He was so much fun when he was well, so handsome and all the girls fancied him. They never believed me when I said we were just friends; it wasn't my business to tell them he was gay, it was up to him.

Dave was a saint on earth as far as I was concerned. He knew me, he loved me, he was always there for me, but now he was gone. I worried about why he hadn't told me he was feeling down in the dumps. I felt I had let him down. I should have noticed if he was feeling low. After all, he was my agony aunt and I was his. Perhaps he, too, had been wearing his 'happy face' the last time I had seen him, the week before he died. Or maybe his faith in the afterlife was greater than mine and he just wanted to get there first. Whatever went on in his mind when he decided to end his life here, I don't think he realised just how much he would be missed.

The fact that I had just lost my best friend did not soften the hearts of Ian's parents. They still refused to allow their son to see me, to cheer me up, so our relationship remained clandestine. Ian felt he was being torn in two directions. He said he loved his family and he loved me, but when they found out four weeks before I had Shannon that he was still seeing me, they told him they would throw him out if he didn't stop seeing me. He told them he wanted to see his child born; they said that was up to him, but that they didn't want to know anything about it.

The stress of the situation caused friction between Ian and me, and we ended up fighting. One night Ian, in a drunken stupor, said some cruel things to me. He said that I had got myself pregnant on purpose, because I was getting on and my looks were fading, and that I had deliberately got pregnant to trap myself a young man. I will never forget those cutting words, especially as they were as far as they could have been from the truth.

We split up two weeks before Shannon was due. In a way, I was relieved it was over because that meant a lot of stress went out of my life. I relished being independent and I enjoyed my own company. I had brought Kelly up without a dad and now she was a lovely thirteen-year-old and would be a great help with the new baby. Shani-Jade would most probably also settle down better if Ian was off the scene, so I made up my mind and let him go.

I didn't try to phone him or go where I knew he would be; I was happy to be alone with my children. A week later, Ian

CAROLINE ROBERTS

began phoning me again, asking if he could pop down and see me, but I knew he was only after sex and that he didn't love me. He didn't really want me, he wanted the baby – he just didn't have the guts to tell me.

I didn't want him anywhere near me, but I didn't want to prevent Shannon from having her dad in her life. I had seen the pain it had caused to Kelly, she longed to get to know her dad, and I too knew firsthand what it felt like. I didn't want Ian, but it was not my place to deny Shannon her father. I told Ian he could come to the birth with my sister Sue, who had been at Shani-Jade's birth too; she was good at calming the fathers down and encouraging me.

On 7 December 1993, Shannon Lacey was born. Ian and I were so relieved that she had no obvious physical abnormalities; in fact, she weighed 6lb 6oz and was very dainty. We were pleased to see that Shannon had a proper little girl's face – no webbed neck, toes or fingers and no pixie features as we had feared! When Shannon came back from being examined, we were told that she had no heart or kidney problems. She was physically perfect. I loved her all the more because of all the worry she had caused me.

All the rejection and bad feelings that I had tolerated because of who my baby's father was all seemed worth it. She was here and well. Tears were in Ian's eyes as he held Shannon for the first time; he told me he was over the moon about her. He went home afterwards and told his parents, 'Caroline had our daughter today and she's beautiful,' but none of them wanted to know. They didn't want to know about their first grandchild; they just rambled on, playing the same old tune about wanting blood tests carried out. Only when the test results were back would they reconsider their feelings on the subject.

I had felt sorry for them at the start of our problems. I knew it must have been hard for them to see that, as they put it, 'Our boy has ruined his life', but now they were rejecting my baby and that made me lose any sympathy I had for them. I didn't even want their precious son any more, but I couldn't get rid of him. He was at my place more than ever. He was overly protective with Shannon and didn't like my other girls picking her up. Inevitably, this caused arguments – and all I wanted was a quiet, peaceful life.

I was supposed to be resting, but I had to do the grocery shopping and carry the heavy bags. Rather than help me out by doing the shopping and carrying the heavy bags, Ian wanted to stay with Shannon and the girls. I ended up with a prolapsed womb from lifting too early after the birth.

The stress of all that had happened throughout 1993 had caused me to lose weight during my pregnancy. Two days after I gave birth to Shannon, I weighed myself and was shocked to find that I weighed two stone less than I had done before I became pregnant.

I looked tired and haggard; my head looked too big for my little body. I'd always wanted to be the weight that I was now, but I looked awful. I was too tired to fight with Ian and ended up drifting back into my relationship with him. He was still telling lies to his family, saying that he was only down seeing the baby. Ian's dad had told me during an argument one day that Ian wasn't interested in me, he was only interested in his baby, and a tiny part of me believed him. I didn't know if Ian was lying when he told me he loved me and I wasn't sure that I loved him, 'cause I certainly didn't trust him. I felt like I had gained two more children rather than having the support of a man around me.

1994

At the start of 1994, I was already feeling low. I was still tearful and grieving for the loss of my dear friend Dave, I was stuck in a relationship I didn't particularly want and I was being pressurised to get a blood test done to prove Ian was Shannon's father.

I was tired all the time. I was not sleeping because of Shannon's night feeds; plus, she was also a very sickly baby. After feeding Shannon, I would rub her back to get her wind up, but what usually came up was a volcanic spraying of milk that would land with pinpoint accuracy over the bedclothes. She would panic when it came through her nostrils. I worried that she might choke on her vomit during the night, so I watched her all the time.

Ian was still very possessive of Shannon and wouldn't let Kelly or Shani-Jade pick her up, but was quite willing to boss them around, getting them to fetch and carry while he held Shannon.

Shani-Jade was being a really naughty girl; she hated Ian being at the house. She became very cheeky and destructive and she argued with Kelly, Ian and me all the time. When Shani-Jade couldn't have her own way, she would get on the phone to her dad crying and he would come round and take her back home for the night. I seemed to have lost all control in my own home. I had asked Dylan if we could all go to family counselling to get help, but he just said that he had no problem with her and that I was the problem.

This was a very unhappy time for me. I just wanted Ian and Dylan to give me some support, but neither did. I wished they would both just stay out of my life; it was easier to be on my own. I didn't need them, but because their respective daughters did I was stuck with them and caught in a trap.

17

RETURN OF THE WESTS

IT WAS 3.15pm, Friday 25 February 1994; I had just got home from picking Shani-Jade up from school. Shannon had thrown up violently in her pram and I was rushing around getting her clean clothes when I heard a news report on the TV that stopped me dead in my tracks and sent a shiver down my spine.

The news report stated that a Gloucester couple had been arrested on suspicion of murdering their sixteen-year-old daughter. The police had been tipped off that the girl was buried under the patio in the rear garden of her parents' home in Cromwell Street.

Straight away, I knew that they were talking about Fred and Rosemary West. I stopped undressing eleven-week-old Shannon, picked her up out of her pram and hugged her close to me. Somehow, being covered in her smelly, milky vomit didn't worry me any more. I sat down on the sofa and tears of anger and sorrow trickled down my face and the bad memories came flooding back.

The report went on to confirm what I already knew: Heather West had disappeared some eight years earlier in 1987 at the age of sixteen. She had never been reported missing. I knew immediately that the tip-off would be right. They would find her under the paving stones of the patio in the rear garden of 25 Cromwell Street. The report went on to say that the police were digging up the garden in their search for Heather.

My head was spinning with mixed emotions – anger, fear and sadness – as my thoughts sped back in time to that night in December 1972 when I had been kept prisoner overnight at 25 Cromwell Street. The shadow of the Wests had darkened my life then, but now, now I was going to make sure that I had the strength and courage I didn't have then. This was a chance to turn my whole life around. Somehow I knew that I would play an important part in securing justice for what had happened to me.

I spoke my thoughts aloud: 'The bastards! How could they kill a child, especially their own child?'

Shani-Jade sat next to me, looking worried. 'What's wrong, Mummy?' I drew her to me and hugged her. Shani-Jade had driven me to the end of my patience in that last year, but I could never hurt her. How could any parent deliberately kill his or her own child?

As I looked down at my dark-haired five-year-old daughter, I remembered two-year-old Heather West, the beautiful toddler with a mop of dark hair and big dark eyes, and I cuddled Shani-Jade to me as I had Heather some 22 years earlier.

When I had calmed down, I phoned Gloucestershire police and told them, 'You have to keep searching, you will find Heather there because that's what they told me they were going to do to me.' I told them what the Wests had threatened to do to me: 'Bury you under the paving stones of Gloucester, there are hundreds of girls there, the police haven't found them and they won't find you.'

As I spoke the words – I will never forget – a nightmare vision came into my head of a mass grave full of young women just like I was at seventeen years old. In the vision, we were all crammed together under the corner of Barton Street; years later, a B&Q shop was built next to it. I could hear us all crying for release from our dark tomb, scratching at the soil around us, trying to claw our way out, our fingers bleeding where we had torn our nails away.

I just hoped the police would take the tip-off seriously. I told them to check the police records and they would find my case. The police told me that they would send two detectives out the next day to see me. When I put the receiver down I sat and sobbed, partly for Heather and partly for myself, as the shame and pain of my past came back to haunt me.

As Kelly came in from school through the back door, I turned my back on her and told her to watch the little ones while I went to the bathroom.

I washed my face and pulled myself together again. I couldn't tell Kelly what had happened, not right then. Poor Kelly had suffered as a direct result of what Rosemary West had done to me. Kelly, too, was a survivor of the Wests; had I not have survived then she wouldn't exist today.

Because of Rose, I hadn't been able to cuddle Kelly since she was ten years old. Since then, I had made her feel rejected and I hated myself for it. It was to be that way throughout her teenage years. I was unable to comfort her with a cuddle when she was hurt or upset because of how it made me feel. The more she needed physical affection from me, the harder it was for me to give it. Eventually she turned to her nan.

The rest of the day was spent reliving that fateful night of 6 December 1972. All the memories of that night came back to haunt me. I felt dirty again, dirty, ashamed and angry. Angry that the Wests were back to the forefront of my mind after all the years of trying to forget that time in my life.

The actual attack came flooding back into my mind; the way the police and the judge had made me feel bad about myself had severely compounded what I was feeling at this time. I thought about the detective that accused me of 'wanting it' because I was no virgin – after all, I'd had sex with two of the lodgers, hadn't I? Well, actually, I hadn't, but when I had explained what had really happened with the lodgers, the detective had just sneered at me as if to say, 'Oh, yeah, tell me another.'

I was angry that the police hadn't taken me seriously when I originally told them about my suspicions in relation to Fred sexually abusing Anna-Marie. Had the police acted all those years ago, and had they informed social services that she was at risk, then I believe that, possibly, it would have saved her from the terrible abuse that, we were to learn of later on, Heather suffered from the age of eight. I wondered if Heather had been used and abused by her parents like I had been.

When Ian called in as usual after work, I broke down as I told him what was going on. I told him, 'They will find her, they will, I know she's dead and I could have been there too!' Ian tried his best to understand, but how could he? He wasn't even born when I was raped, he couldn't take it in. He knew I had been raped, he knew a woman had forced herself on to me sexually. I had told him about the Wests when we had come across certain problems in our sexual relationship, but it was not something I would go into too much detail about, as I found it very upsetting and embarrassing.

Ian went home for his tea, as usual, while I got a take-away for the girls and me. Shani-Jade's dad called by to see her and when he left she started being naughty. I couldn't cope with her so I ranted and raved at her and put her to bed out of the way.

Later on that night, Ian came back and helped by bathing Shannon and settling her down in her pram in the living room. Once the kids were asleep, I tried to relax and watch a video with Ian, but it was hard to concentrate with all the other things going through my mind.

I sat down and armed myself with a pen and paper and began to write down everything that I could remember about the Wests and the night they abducted me. It took me a few hours and it disturbed and distressed me, but it helped to clear my mind some. I decided it would be easier for me to give the police my written account to work from, as it would save me some embarrassment.

I didn't mention the part about the lodgers. I didn't see how it would be of any help to the police; after all, it was the Wests they were investigating, not me. And besides, I didn't want to face all that shame again.

Mum phoned to tell me about the news report, and I told her I already knew and that the police were coming to interview me. Mum was, understandably, upset at this. She said, 'Do you think he has killed her?' I told her that I believed so, and that it was what they had threatened to do to me. Mum went all quiet, then said, 'That could have been you, Caroline, you are so lucky.' I could feel the tears welling inside me, so I made my excuses and told Mum I would phone her back the next day, after the police had gone.

At 1.45pm on 26 February 1994, DC Jeff Morgan and DC Barbara Harrison came to take a statement from me. I gave them what I had written, told them that I found it hard to talk about it, and asked them if we could work from what I had written. That's what we did. I answered their other questions as well as I could. I recalled everything that was done to me, but little things like which room the two little ones had slept in hadn't stuck in my mind.

At 5.20pm, the police left with an eleven-page statement and a new insight into the personalities of both Fred and Rose West, an insight that had shocked them. As they left, they told me that they couldn't check my statement of 1972 because they didn't have records from that far back. They thanked me for my time and said they were sorry I had to go through it again. This time, the police were human, not like back in the seventies.

Later that night, Superintendent John Bennett gave a televised press release. The police had found human bones in the

Wests' garden, and Rose West had been arrested too. I spoke out aloud: 'Those bastards, they've killed Heather, and there will be more, I know there will. They killed before they had me, there will be more!' Ian gave me a strange look as I added, 'And what are they doing about the black men and the sex circle? I wonder if they've found them.'

I must have sounded like crazy woman; Ian had no idea what I was ranting on about. I hadn't told him about them, same as I hadn't told him about the lodgers. I had never told anyone about the lodgers, and the thought of it coming out was making me ill, just as it had 22 years earlier.

Mum phoned me. 'Did you see the news report, Caroline? It seems they have found her.' She sounded tearful as she repeated what she had already said earlier. 'My God, Caroline, it could have been you, you are so lucky!' She offered to come over the next day to help me with the children, but I lied and said I was fine. I said I would call over and see her instead.

I cried myself to sleep that night, and when I slept my long-standing nightmare came back to haunt me. I was under the paving stones, calling for my mum to help me, trapped in my dark, dank grave under the noisy pavement next to the train track on the Barton Street crossing. I was also having nightmares about Heather; I saw her being abused as I had been, by her parents.

The police had told me that Anna-Marie was safe, and I recollected that I had seen her in the Beer Keller, in Westgate Street, back in 1983. She was sat in the company of Rose and two dubious-looking men, drinking and chatting away happily. I had been there on a hen night with thirty other girls when I spotted Rose.

I had to leave before she saw me, but I did speak to Anna-Marie in the Ladies. She was about eighteen years old and had turned out a chubby girl. I asked her if her name was Anna and she said, 'Yes, do you know my mum?' I said I had known her years ago, and she sweetly said, 'Why don't you come and say hello,' but I told her I had to leave and we all went on to another pub. Seeing Rose again had startled me, but at least I could see Anna was OK, though I did wonder if she was on the game.

I had seen Fred once since the assault too. In 1988, Sue had driven me to Gloucester and we parked in the car park at the end of Cromwell Street, though we took a different route. At first I didn't recognise the place, but as we got out of the car I saw Fred.

He was wearing a donkey jacket and was carrying some DIY items under his arm while smiling to himself. As soon as I saw him, I ducked down and hid behind Suzanne's car.

She said, 'What are you doing?'

I told her, 'Get down, it's Fred West!'

She looked around and spotted him – he was only two cars away! As he passed, he smiled at her.

Sue said, 'I'm not scared of the bastard.'

I told her, 'Well I am! Please, Sue, don't say anything to him.'

I was petrified he would see me and threaten me, but he didn't see me squatting down behind the car and went on towards his home, whistling as he strutted, as cocky as ever.

That night, I couldn't sleep for thinking of him so I looked up his number in the phone book, and at 2.00am I rang his number. A soft-voiced woman answered – it wasn't Rose. I think it may have been Anna-Marie or possibly Fred's daughter Mae, who had just been a babe in arms the last time I had seen her. I didn't speak; I waited a minute in silence and then put the phone down.

Half an hour later, I phoned again, hoping to get him to the phone. I didn't want to say anything, I just wanted to disturb his sleep, like he had mine over the years, but when the girl's voice answered the phone again, I put the handset down and never called that number again.

Now he was back and his shadow was disturbing my sleep again. I knew he was dangerous, but even what he and Rose had done to me, and threatened to do to me, hadn't prepared me for what was about to be discovered.

I found out, much later, that Fred had already confessed to Heather's murder before the police had interviewed me on the Saturday, and that he had been taken back to 25 Cromwell Street on the Friday evening, while Rose was being questioned at Cheltenham Police Station, to point out where he had buried Heather. The police had already started digging in another spot and Fred told them they were digging in the wrong place.

At 4.00pm on that Saturday, 26 February 1994, a thigh bone was discovered buried by the back door of the house, some distance from the area where Fred had told them to search for Heather.

At first, it was thought that it might have been a bone from an ancient Roman burial site, as Gloucester was built on such a burial site. The thigh bone was taken away for forensic examination.

Later that day, the police found what was later identified as Heather's remains. Her body had been cut up, her head and legs removed and squashed in next to her torso, in a hole which was only one foot across. After the first thigh bone had been examined, the police knew they were looking at two sets of remains.

It wasn't an act of remorse or conscience that had made Fred confess and aid the police in their search for Heather, it was a calculated risk he had taken to stop further bodies being discovered. He thought that if he admitted to killing Heather during a heated argument then he could get off with a lighter sentence.

When police put it to Fred that Heather was not the only murder victim buried in his garden, and told him they had discovered a second set of remains, Fred realised that his plan had failed. The police were going to dig up every inch of his garden and Fred knew what they would find, so he confessed that there were two more bodies buried there.

On Sunday 27 February 1994, Fred was taken back to his home to point out the burial site of an eighteen-year-old ex-tenant and lover of his, Shirley Robinson. At the time of her death, Shirley was heavily pregnant with Fred's child; the tiny skeleton was found next to that of its mother's.

Fred also pointed out to the police the site where he had buried sixteen-year-old Alison Chambers. As the days went by, I listened to every news item covering the investigation. The story was constantly in the news that week and on the front pages of every newspaper. There was worldwide media interest and a large crowd of journalists began congregating outside 25 Cromwell Street. Each day, a new set of human remains was found.

By 8 March 1994, Fred had admitted to killing twelve girls. Nine of these girls were buried at 25 Cromwell Street, some beneath the garden, some underneath the cellar floor and some under the walls. Two more, his ex-wife and another pregnant ex-lover, were buried in two adjacent fields in Kemply, near the cottage he was raised in. At the former home of Fred and Rose, 25 Midland Road, another victim was found buried under the kitchen floor.

It was hard to take in. How could they have done such vile and repulsive things? How could they have got away with it for so long? The murders spanned a period of three decades – surely someone must have been suspicious? Worst of all was the fact that Fred's eight-year-old stepdaughter Charmaine West was one of the victims. They had killed her before the attack on me; how come I was allowed to live while an innocent child was not?

I couldn't sleep properly. I watched TV all day so I wouldn't miss any of the news reports. Each body recovered added to my guilt as I blamed myself for not pressing ahead with the rape charges when I had had the chance. There was no consolation in my self-recrimination other than the fact that I was still alive. I could only think that had I pressed ahead against the Wests then most of the victims would still be alive. My stance in not pursuing the Wests seems to have given them a licence to kill, kill and kill again and again. Within months of my case going to court, in 1973, two girls were murdered! These two girls were wanted and loved by their parents, and their siblings didn't despise them.

One of the two girls, Linda Gough, would most certainly have survived if Fred had been put away for raping me. Linda was killed in April 1973, just three months after the Wests were found guilty of assaulting me. It was Linda's death I held myself mostly responsible for, but I felt that all the others had died because of me too. If only I had pressed the rape charge, Fred and Rose would have been thought of as dangerous and the police would have suspected them when Linda had gone missing. Linda would have lived if Fred was locked up. Even after he was released, he would have been a suspect when hitchhikers and young girls waiting for buses disappeared in the area.

Fred's fear of Rose had been so great that he had to let me go but, because I told the police, he wasn't going to risk letting any of his future victims go free. I had sentenced them to death.

While every one hugged me and said how lucky I was to be alive, all I could think of was how terribly guilty I felt having survived.

18

MEDIA FRENZY

ON 9 MARCH 1994, a knock came at the door and there stood two men dressed in Wellington boots and Barbour jackets. They looked like farmers.

I had just picked Kelly, her two schoolmates, Shani-Jade and Shannon up from school. The house was noisy with children chattering and coats were strewn all over the place. Before I could ask who they were, Kelly had let them. Once inside, they introduced themselves as Andrew Parker, the staff reporter from the *Sun* newspaper, and Phil Haviland, a photographer.

Andrew did most of the talking. He started off by saying what a lucky escape I had had from the Wests. I was surprised they knew about me, as I had only helped the police with their inquiries and I was sure the police wouldn't have told the *Sun* about me. He went on to say that he knew all about what had happened to me in 1972 and that he could write a story on it there and then, but that he needed to hear my account of what had happened to me at the hands of the Wests so that the facts were right.

I told him I had nothing to say, as I didn't want any publicity, but he explained that even if I didn't want to be identified and got a court order taken out to stop the press writing about me, it was too big a story and someone would take the risk and publish it, with or without my permission or help. At that time, no one was really to know how big the news would be on the sinister goings on at Cromwell Street. In my mind, I simply wanted to put an 'X' in the box marked 'No Publicity'.

I couldn't believe what was happening. I dreaded all my secrets being published for everyone worldwide to read about. I said that, as a rape victim, they had no right to publish my identity, but Andrew said someone would do it, so why didn't I give them an 'exclusive'? That way I would have control over what was published and they would pay me for it. He told me to think of it as a form of compensation. I presumed he was right – that way I could have some control over the story and explain what had really happened.

I didn't know what my rights were. I was on benefits and I had no money for legal help and, besides, I felt that if I didn't agree with the two men from the *Sun* they would go ahead and publish what they did know, which would have been what they had learned from the 1973 court case as written in the *Gloucestershire Citizen*. This had made it look as though I had co-operated with the Wests and I didn't want that coming up again, so here was my chance to put the record straight and, as well as that, here was a man willing to pay me for the truth.

The guilt I was feeling about letting the Wests get away with it before had made me determined that I would not do or say anything that would give the Wests' solicitor any excuse to say that the media had made it impossible for the Wests to have a fair trial. That might allow them to get away with their crimes once again.

I felt I owed it to those poor girls to help get the Wests convicted this time. My pride had got in the way last time, but I had grown up and matured mentally a lot since then and I felt I had to behave responsibly and get justice for the girls that didn't make it.

I asked Andrew, how they had found out about me. They surprised me when they said my old boyfriend Tony Coates had spoken to them. They said that Tony hadn't been able to eat or sleep, worrying that Fred had killed me and that I was one of those yet-to-be-identified bodies. Tony had gone to Cromwell Street and asked them to find out if I was still alive. All he knew was that I lived somewhere in Cinderford and he hadn't seen me for twenty years.

I told them I would have to think about it, adding that my partner would be in soon and he would not be happy to find them in my home. As I said it, Ian came in. When I introduced them as reporters from the *Sun*, Ian gave them a dirty look and walked out of the room. They left saying they would be back the next day to see what I had decided.

When the reporters had gone, Ian and I had an almighty row about them being in the house. He said I shouldn't have let them in or spoken to them; he wanted me to have nothing to do with them.

Later that evening, I phoned Tony Coates. I had not been in communication with Tony for twenty years. He was so happy to hear from me – he really had thought I was dead. I asked him why he had thought such a thing. He said that he had seen Fred and Rose in a pub about two years after they had assaulted me; he followed them outside when they left and started giving Fred a beating.

A group of men, who were on their way into the pub, dragged Tony off Fred thinking he was the bad guy, and then gave Tony a kicking. As they pulled Tony off Fred, Fred sneered at Tony and said, 'She's dead, mate. She's dead.' When Fred said this, he was laughing at Tony.

Tony said he didn't think anything of it at the time – he thought it was just Fred being a bastard – but when the unidentified bodies started surfacing, he thought I was one of them, so he asked a reporter to find out if I was still alive.

They found me through my maiden name in the phone book by tracing my brother Phillip. They went to his old address and the neighbours there told them where Phillip worked. They phoned him at work and asked for my address and Phillip gave it to them.

Later that evening, I got a message via Wendy, the sister of the late Dave Reed. The message said that her friend, who worked at the local *Forester* newspaper, had said two local people had been in separately to break the news that there was a local woman that had been raped by Fred West. They were most likely hoping for a small reward for their information, but the paper had decided it was too big a story for them to publish. Moreover, they only printed once a week and they expected the national press would soon be on to me, so they decided to forewarn me that people were trying to leak my name to the press. I guess I owed them one.

I spoke to their reporter, Mike Tonge, over the phone and asked him to help me deal with the big boys from the *Sun*. Mike gave me what legal advice he could, and was with me when I spoke to them the next day.

They had arrived by ten o'clock. There was some chit-chat about money and they offered me £500 for an exclusive and photos. Even I knew that wasn't a fair offer. They expected me to tell the world all the disgusting things that I had gone through for the same amount they had paid for one old photo of Fred, or to use a room in Cromwell Street to photograph the dig scene with its tarpaulin. This wasn't chequebook journalism, not as far as I was concerned. In retrospect, I guess Andrew could have offered me the top figure he had in mind straight away without first trying to catch me with a minnow of a figure.

Mike told them that they couldn't expect me to ruin my home life and give up my privacy for a paltry amount. They said that if we went exclusive with them that they could keep all the other newspapers off my back, and that it wouldn't be long till I would be besieged with media people and would become a prisoner in my own home, a prediction that was to ring true.

The *Sun* wanted to know some more about the story I had to tell, and I gave them seven pages of the eight-page account that I had originally written out for the police, and for the same reason – I found it all too embarrassing to talk about. The men from the *Sun* said it would be better if I went public and allowed them to photograph me too. They went on to remind me,

'Someone somewhere will sell your photo to the newspapers and other papers will publish it without getting the true story; it's too big a story to miss.' I was still maintaining that I didn't want to be identified; I didn't think I could cope with everyone knowing what had happened to me.

Having thought about it I decided that if it was all going to come out anyway, then there was nothing wrong in me accepting payment for it. At least that way I could be the one who put my side of the story across, rather than some interfering busybody who knew nothing of what had really happened to me or the long-term effect it had had on my life.

Andrew Parker from the *Sun* went out to use his mobile phone to see how much he could offer me and when he came back in, he said, 'The editor says £10,000.' That was a lot of money to me, but I still didn't know whether to trust them or not. I had held back page five of the written account till then – not to make more money from it (as I was later accused of) but because it contained the most degrading and humiliating details of the assault and I didn't want them seeing those until I had their word that my story would not be published until the trial of Fred and Rose West was over. They agreed to my terms and I, in return, accepted their offer.

Andrew Parker's mobile phone rang and he tipped me off that the rest of the media was on its way from Gloucester to find me. Immediately I felt a sense of panic; I couldn't cope with having the press fighting over me on my doorstep right there on the High Street. The pair from the *Sun* said they would take me away from the house for a while. I ended up leaving baby Shannon with my brother Rob and his partner

Lyn. I asked them to collect Shani-Jade from school and phone Kelly's school to tell her not to go home but to go to their house instead.

I went in the clothes I had on, expecting to be back later in the day, but they took me eight miles away to the Chase Hotel in nearby Ross-on-Wye, a very nice, posh hotel and one that I felt completely out of place in. On the way there we stopped because Phil wanted a photo of me to send to the editor. He got me to sit on a stile with a field behind it. As he began to focus his camera, a woman pushed three people in wheelchairs into the field, one by one, and lined them up. She then proceeded to start digging a hole while the three in the wheelchairs watched. It just seemed so weird and, I'm afraid to say, it made me laugh. I felt really bad that I had found it funny, but I couldn't help myself. Maybe it was my sense of humour or maybe it was my nerves, I don't know. It turned out that the lady was planting trees – there was nothing more sinister to it than that – but it was certainly not a suitable backdrop for a photo of one of the Wests' surviving victims.

I was kept in the hotel room and I was not allowed to let any of my family know where I was, as the press would pressurise them into telling them my whereabouts and that would cause problems for both me and the *Sun* men.

Meanwhile, Ian had called at my home and gone out searching for me. He went to Rob's and all Rob knew was that I had gone off with two men to hide from the media. Rob told Ian he thought the men might be the police or reporters.

Ian phoned the police and found out they didn't have me, so he phoned the *Sun* news desk and got very angry and upset that they wouldn't tell him where I was. He threatened to talk to the other newspapers if they didn't let him talk to me. Eventually, they phoned Andrew Parker's mobile and allowed me to talk to him. He was very upset and insisted I tell him where I was, but I was not allowed to. I told him not to worry and asked Andrew Parker what time he thought I would be going home. He said it would be best to stay away overnight.

I was not expecting to have to be away that long, but agreed. Ian was not a happy chappy about it. I told him I would ask Rob to keep the girls overnight, but Ian wasn't having any of it. He said he would take Shannon home with him. I tried to talk Ian out of having Shannon at his parents' home. At that time Shannon was three months old and Ian's parents had never seen her, let alone wanted her in their home.

My future sister-in-law, Lynne, had a baby two weeks older than Shannon and was used to her, plus she had all the equipment there. Ian only had the carrycot and bottles that I had left at Lynne's, but he was obstinate and wouldn't change his mind, so I gave in and told him he could take Shannon home as long as his parents were OK about it.

Ian calmed down and said to come home as soon as possible. He then told his mum what had happened and told her he was taking his daughter home to their place to sleep. Later, Ian told me that he took Shannon in and straight up to his room where he cared for her all night; his parents never set eyes on her.

The next morning, he took Shannon back to Rob's and went to work, while I had some more photos taken and was given a £2,000 advance payment from the *Sun* – the rest would be paid on publication of my story.

Andrew Parker advised me that I should go and stay with my sister Sue, as she lived in a country lane near Newland, on the outskirts of Coleford, seven miles away from my home in Cinderford. He drove me there and said I was not to let anyone know where I was and not to answer the phone.

I hated putting on Sue, but she was happy to let me stay. I was missing Shannon so much that I asked Ian to meet me at Sue's with her. I spoke to Shani-Jade and Kelly over the phone and told them not to worry and that I would be with them on the following Sunday.

On the Sunday night, under the cover of darkness, I sneaked home, having been gone since the Thursday morning. On the way, I collected my two other girls. The phone kept ringing, but we couldn't answer it in case it was the press, so we ignored it.

The next day, my friend Julie came down and, very kindly, took Shani-Jade to school and even picked her back up for me. During the day, Julie spent the day with me, answering the phone and telling any press that called that I was away, that she was babysitting and that I didn't want to speak to any of them. All week Julie did the shopping, the school run and continued to answer the phone. Eventually, I bought an answering machine to screen the calls.

The neighbours were being questioned about me; TV and press reporters were knocking on their doors all day long. There were reporters in their droves asking about me in pubs and clubs but, luckily for me, the people they spoke to who knew me maintained a wall of silence.

I had the press sat outside my house and photographers parked in the car park opposite with cameras at the ready. In the first week, I couldn't leave the house and my poor old mum had reporters asking her questions. Mum let some of the news-hungry reporters into her home; they rewarded her – behind her back, while she made them a cup of tea – by taking a photo of a photo that hung on Mum's wall of me and Kelly, which had been taken ten years earlier. Mum and I had an argument about her talking to the press. She didn't know they were just interested in the news value of my story; she thought they were concerned about her beautiful daughter.

At the end of the week, Ian, Rob, Lynne and I went away to Butlins holiday complex at Minehead for a weekend. We had booked it up months before, and now it seemed like a blessing to be able to get away and not worry about the press.

We had a great time and I felt a lot better for being away from home and the probing eyes of the media. When we got back, it seemed to be worse than ever. Even more victims' remains were being recovered and identified. Their photographs were plastered all over the newspapers. It had been hard enough knowing they had been murdered, but putting the faces to the victims made it more real and hammered it home. I felt guiltier than ever.

The press were still skulking around all day. Some stayed outside my house all evening. I missed Kelly's award night at school because reporters were parked outside my home, which was upsetting for both of us. Kelly wanted to go out to them and tell them to go away and leave her mum alone, but I told her to ignore them. She also had to come home via the neighbours' and sneak in over the picket fence at the back of the house.

There was one very dogged reporter from the *Sunday Mirror*

who deserved a medal for his persistence. He had left his card and number on my door mat. This man was one of the reporters who was asking about me in the pubs and clubs and talking to the neighbours and my mum about me. The problem was that I'd signed up with the *Sun* and if I even so much as whimpered at another journalist, I would not get the remainder of the promised fee.

This *Sunday Mirror* reporter, Howard Souness, had won my mum around and even managed to use his skills to get her to ask me to talk to him, which, obviously, I refused to do. Every time he called, I hid and wouldn't open the door to him. He had called several times in one day and I ended up climbing my neighbour's fence while still wet from my bath, along with Shannon, the two of us wrapped only in bath towels. I hid at my neighbour's for half an hour and then sneaked back around home when he had gone.

I did manage to go out visiting the family one night, but it was under the cover of darkness and in disguise: hooded coat, long wig and spectacles. I looked hideous, but not even my friends recognised me.

It was a good thing that I had a good sense of humour, 'cause I certainly needed it at times. One night, Julie came round to spend the evening with me and answer the door to reporters. We shared a bottle of wine and were getting quite tipsy when she decided to pop next door to the shop in the garage to get some cigarettes. A few minutes later, when I was still wearing my long dark wig, I heard a knock at the door. Thinking it was Julie back from the garage, I opened the door for her as I passed it on my way to the bathroom. I got a shock: standing there was a good-looking young man with short dark hair. Even before he told me his name, I knew from Mum's description that it was the *Sunday Mirror* reporter.

I stood there open-mouthed for a second as he said, 'Hello, are you Caroline? I'm Howard Souness.'

This had taken me aback and I wasn't sure what to do as we stood there looking at each other. I started speaking in broken English, 'No, sorry. Caroleen, Mrs Owens [as I was then], she is no here, she gone. She no want to see people. I babysit, I au pair.'

I thought my wig and accent had done the trick. Then he asked, 'When will Caroline be back?'

Before I could answer, I heard a very curt voice boom out from behind him. We both jumped!

Julie was back. She bellowed, 'Excuse me, young man! Who are you and what do you want?' She was good at being bossy.

Howard looked nervous and turned to see where the voice had suddenly come from. He looked like a naughty schoolboy that had been caught doing something he shouldn't be.

I called past him to Julie, again in my foreign accent, 'Dees man, he name Howhard Siness, he wanna Caroleen.'

Howard introduced himself to Julie, who I could see had caught on to what I was up to and was trying not to laugh. I had to run upstairs and leave Julie to deal with him on the doorstep, because I was dying to laugh and nearly peed my pants. I went to the bathroom and then sat on the landing listening to Julie quizzing the poor reporter.

He asked Julie, 'Are you Caroline?'

Julie answered in a snooty tone, 'That, young man, is my business. Maybe I am, maybe I am not. What are you after?'

THE ONE THAT GOT AWAY

Then she changed tack and added, 'Maybe I am a police officer here to see that Mrs Owens is not harassed by the media. You are aware, are you not, that you would be breaking the law if you publish anything about Mrs Owens' ordeal? You are aware, are you not, that the Attorney General has forbidden any part of Mrs Owens' business to do with the West investigation being published?'

Then she added, 'I suggest, young man, that you go away and leave Mrs Owens alone.'

'So are you working for the police?' he said.

Julie said, 'I am going to close the door now, young man. If you don't go, I will have to be rude and shut it in your face, and I don't like being rude, so will you please go? I will tell Mrs Owens you called. Goodbye!' And with that, she shut the door on him.

It was so funny. Julie should have got an Oscar for that performance, she really cheered me up. My own quick thinking impressed me too; the Spanish au pair just came from nowhere. I was just glad he didn't talk back to me in Spanish; I'd have been stuck then.

Another day, the men from the *Sun* came to see me; they said they had spotted a photographer from the *Star* newspaper watching the house, so Julie decided we would get rid of him by using her as a decoy.

From a past newspaper feature, Julie knew that a woman from our local branch of Lloyds Bank had been paid £50,000 compensation by a newspaper for publishing her photo in an article saying she was Rose West. Julie thought she might get a few quid if they put her picture in under my name, and it would serve them right for pestering me. Julie took Shannon for a walk up the town in her pram, while the two *Sun* men and I watched from behind my nets. As Julie left through the front door, the *Star* man was out of his car and heading up a short cut behind the street, camera hidden in his jacket.

He was running because he needed to get in front of Julie. Ten minutes later he came running back to his car, a big smile on his face; happy that he had got the photo he had waited all day for.

When Julie came back, she told us how he was trying to keep his camera out of sight and how she kept stopping to fiddle with the baby's covers and looking up and smiling a lot, as she said hello to everyone she passed that she vaguely knew so he could get a good shot, all the time pretending she hadn't seen him.

We had a good laugh about it, but the next day, as I carried Shannon round to the garage shop next door, he was back! I came out of the garage with my arms full of shopping, struggling to hold Shannon when I spotted him blocking my way, so I waited in the garage a while.

A taxi pulled in for petrol. I rushed out and paid the driver to take me round to the back of my place; some fifty yards away. The photographer chased after us and tried to take my picture. As I ran down my back path, I shouted at him, 'Leave me alone or I'll call the police!'

He shouted back to me to pose for him and called out, 'The sooner I get your photo, the sooner I'm out of here!' Then he went back to his car, phoned me from his mobile and said, 'Why don't you just let me get a photo of you by your car? You don't have to pose.' He said that his editor had told him he couldn't leave till he got a photo of me and that he had kids to support and he needed his job. He was using emotional blackmail on me. I told him to tell his editor to go to hell and slammed the phone down. I then watched him from behind my bedroom nets; he made a phone call and drove off.

Even though I was under contract to the *Sun*, it didn't put an end to the offers I was getting from other newspapers. Even the good-looking Howard Souness caught up with me in the end, so I gave in and let him in. He seemed a nice man, just as Mum had said he was, but he was after the same thing: my story and photo.

He offered me £50,000 to go to the *Sunday Mirror* instead. It was a lot of money, but the stress caused by the gagging clause in the *Sun* contract was bad enough and I didn't need any more stress. I knew these reporters were just doing a job, but I was now on my own in having to defend my right to silence, otherwise my contract with the *Sun* wouldn't be worth the paper it was written on and they would have the right to cancel the contract.

Andrew Parker and his editor from the *Sun* then told me that my mum had told my story to two other newspapers and that it would jeopardise my contract with them. I had another argument with Mum about that – and afterwards, naturally, I felt bad about it.

That evening, Andrew Parker came to see me, but I was exhausted with stress and didn't get to see him. I was over at Rob's house and needed a rest from it all. I didn't want some stupid contract ruining my relationship with my mum. In May

1994, I had a meeting with Andrew Parker and a colleague to sort our differences out.

I was ageing fast from all the stress and guilt that I was feeling, plus I had to cope with my sick child, my naughty child and a boyfriend that was no more than a child himself. I just couldn't do it; I had too much going on in my head to add to it, even if it was for £40,000 more!

Yes, I needed money; I had just left my husband and the house and its contents and was living in private rented property. I had no furniture, washer or cooker of my own and I was struggling to make ends meet. I needed the money to replace everything I had left behind, but that's all I needed and £10,000 would cover that and leave me something to put towards saving for Shannon to have IVF treatment, if and when she decided she wanted children.

I wasn't greedy; I didn't need £50,000 and the added stress of two newspapers fighting over me.

19

SPOKEN WORDS
COULD NOT SAY

THE POLICE CAME round to see me again, wanting to ask me more questions. They said they had interviewed one of my ex-boyfriends, Steve Riddall – the sailor I had been out with years before – about the night he had stayed in the Wests' house. The police said he had told me to, 'Get away from the Wests, they're not right!' He had also bragged that he had given me my first ever orgasm. A *Sun* reporter told me later that Steve Riddall had been phoning around the newspapers trying to sell his story of his night of passion with a surviving West victim. Gallantly, they all turned him down. Ouch! That must have hurt his ego!

One day, DC Jeff Morgan asked me if there was anything else I could tell him about my time with the Wests. Was there anything I had found too hard to talk about? I knew that he knew about the lodgers and what had happened, and I knew if I didn't tell him about them he would not be able to rely on me to tell the truth, but I couldn't tell him face to face, so I just smiled and said, 'If I think of something, I'll let you know.'

I had never told a soul about the attempted rape at Cromwell Street, as I had felt dirty and ashamed of that episode ever since. I was afraid that those who supposedly loved me might not love me if they knew the truth of what had happened with them.

That night, after Ian had gone home, I stayed up late and wrote down everything about the lodgers that my spoken words could not express and, the following morning, I mailed it to DC Morgan. I explained that I'd had sex with Ben on the floor of their bedsit and that, later, I had fallen asleep and woken to find the visitor trying to have sex with me. I explained that I had told him to get off and that he was verbally abusive towards me.

Seeing it written down that way, it didn't seem so bad and, going by today's standards, it was nothing to be ashamed of. I know quite a few girls here in Cinderford who have been in threesomes with married couples or have been with more than one man in one day. Cinderford also has its own very attractive lesbian who seems to have converted a good dozen young woman to bisexuality. And they talk about it openly as if it's just another of life's experiences, not something to make you feel repulsed or bad about yourself.

So, feeling a little better about myself, the next day I went to see Sue, Julie and Ian, all individually, and told them I had something to tell them that I had felt bad about for twenty-odd years and that I hoped wouldn't make them think less of me. After I had told them my story, they all said it made no difference and that I shouldn't have ever worried about it. I felt a lot better after getting that off my chest.

The day after DC Morgan received my letter, he came back to see me again and I apologised for not telling him sooner. He said he understood and I made another statement about the lodgers.

He came to see me again to show me some brown parcel tape and asked if I recognised it as the tape the Wests had used to gag me in the car. I recognised it and made a statement saying it was the same kind of tape.

I also had to make a statement about the black men I had seen at the house. I knew the name of one of them, Roy, the smiley-faced man who had helped me to leave the Wests and had taken me home once. He had told the police how he had rescued me and had never gone back to 25 Cromwell Street again.

By April 1994, Rose West had been charged with the rape and assault of a twelve-year-old girl and a seven-year-old boy. Up until then, she had been staying in a safe house and I had worried she might send her 'black friends' to silence me. I had received several silent phone calls while she was in the safe house and worried that it was either her or one of her 'black friends'. DC Morgan assured me that she didn't have that kind of clout.

Rose was charged with one murder, then two more and was locked up on remand awaiting trial.

20

'I WAS FRED WEST'S SEX SLAVE'

IN APRIL 1994, I went through a really bad patch of depression. I was constantly arguing with Dylan over Shani-Jade's behaviour. Ian and I were still seeing each other in secret, even though by now we had got the blood test result back – proving Ian to be Shannon's dad. His family accepted Shannon, but still they wanted Ian to have nothing to do with me. So he was only allowed to come down to my house to spend time with Shannon.

He started taking Shannon up to his parents' house on Sundays for the afternoon and they fell in love with her. I was happy for Ian and Shannon, but hurt that they wouldn't give me a chance.

The pressure of the press and the police investigations and not being able to go out anywhere with Ian was getting me down. I was hitting out at the ones I loved. I didn't want Ian touching me; I felt even more that he was just using me for his own pleasure, just as 'they' had. I now had names and faces to the victims of the Wests and started having vivid dreams about some of them and their deaths.

Fred had told the police, during interviews, that I hadn't put up much of a fight and that if I hadn't said I would go back to his home to live, he wouldn't have let me go and he would have killed me.

Then to top it all, the police told me I might be able to testify in court against the Wests, something I hadn't expected. I thought that the courts were not allowed to bring up previous offences. I was in turmoil about it; I didn't know if I would be able to cope. Knowing that everyone would read of my past in the press was bad enough, but to be called up in front of a judge and jury and have the watching world dissect every detail was too much for me to deal with. I didn't know if I would be able to tell each disgusting detail and then be able to take being torn apart by some sarcastic defence barrister. My hair began to fall out and I had big bald patches all over my head.

I went up the pub and got very drunk, then bawled my eyes out. The next day, I went to the doctor and was prescribed anti-depressants. I talked to my health visitor about it and she asked me to consider counselling. I gave it some thought and decided it might help, so she fixed me up with a counsellor from Gloucester.

On my way to my first session, in Stroud Road, Gloucester, I took the first turning left instead of the second and found myself in a dead-end street. I was lost, so when I saw a policeman coming out from one of the big townhouses I pulled up next to the house to ask him the way.

When another policeman came out of the house behind him, it suddenly hit me that I was outside 25 Midland Road, where they had recently recovered the body of little Charmaine West! It completely freaked me out. I put my foot down and drove away like a mad woman. I found my way to the counsellor's office and broke down crying.

I went for counselling every week for fourteen weeks, but each time it got harder and harder for me, as I was remembering more and more of what had been done to me and what I had done to others as a child. It was painful.

The day before a counselling session, I would be bad tempered and moody and I would try to be at least ten minutes late getting there so I wouldn't have so long with my counsellor. I spent my time in these therapy sessions talking about my problems with Shani-Jade and Ian and his parents, instead of talking about the rape or my childhood. I hated being there and in the end I just stopped going.

Eventually, Ian's parents found out he had been deceiving them and that we were still an item, and, in their frustration, they threw him out and he moved in with me. When Ian moved in with me, Shani-Jade moved out. I had done my best to keep her, but she was adamant she wanted to live with her dad. In October 1994, I reluctantly let her go. It was really upsetting for me as I felt I had failed her. I secretly hoped she would come back after a couple of months, but she didn't.

Moving in with her dad meant that Shani-Jade was happier and I still got to take her to and from school every day and have her whenever she had time off school, plus weekends, so it worked out well for all concerned in the end.

At long last, by November 1994, Ian's parents, realising that he had made his choice about his daughter and me, gave in and I was accepted into their family fold. Weeks later, they offered to sell us their house at a lower price than it was valued at, so we could afford it.

I first met Ian's family after his grandmother's funeral. They were all very nice and polite towards me and tried to make me feel welcome. I could see that they loved Shannon very much and I felt they were sorry that it had taken them so long to make their peace with me, though that was never talked about.

Almost immediately, Ian set about buying his family's house for us, as I needed to move due to lots of TV and newspaper people getting on to me – they wanted to prepare programmes and documentaries for post-trial coverage. We would drive past and see them sat in their cars, watching the house, hoping to catch me in, but I spent more time at Ian's parents' home. They had quickly moved into their new home, and we lived at both Albion Place and Latimer Road during December.

Before 1994 was over, I was to lose another friend – Nicky Bowers, my karaoke mentor. This was the man who first got me singing with his karaoke and gave me the confidence to sing in public. Nicky was such a happy, outgoing person and everybody liked him. In December 1994, Nicky hanged himself in his home. No one knew he was down. He didn't show it, a bit like me really. People knew him for his happy-go-lucky personality. Even when something was hurting him, he had to keep up his pretence of happiness. The stress of it all drove him to kill himself in such a cruel way. He was only in his early thirties. I wondered what must have been going through his mind as he was putting the noose around his head; he must have been so sad and desperate to do that.

The death of Nicky left a lot of people very upset and everyone that knew him was shocked. I had already endured the loss of Dave Reed, which had led me to the conclusion that we never really know what is going on in each other's minds. The local church of St Stephens was packed out to capacity for Nicky's funeral. One question remained unanswered: why? When one of Nicky's closest friends, Jabber, stood up and sang 'Don't Let The Sun Go Down On Me', everybody in the church was in tears and even the local hard men broke down.

Christmas '94 I spent at Albion Place. Mum and Shani-Jade came round for lunch and members of my family dropped in during the afternoon. In the evening, we took Kelly and Shannon to Ian's parents for a party, while Dylan and Shani-Jade went off to visit Dylan's family in Liverpool.

1995

Nicky's death, coming as it did so near to Christmas, was still raw in my mind when I got a phone call from a *Today* reporter telling me that Fred West was dead. He had, I was told, hanged himself on New Year's Day, 1995, in his prison cell. The *Today* man asked me what I thought. I said I was shocked and that I didn't think he would kill himself. I thought, with Fred in court knowing he was not going to be set free again, he might tell us everything he had done. He was a braggart, he wouldn't be able to keep it in, he would have to share it with someone, either the courts or his son Stephen, or at least a fellow prisoner. I had hoped we would find all the other victims he had allegedly killed, including Mary Bastholme, a sixteen-year-old who went missing in 1968.

Now I was being told he had made his escape. I said to the reporter that I felt sorry for his children because, after all, he was still their dad, whom they loved whatever he had done to them and others. I felt especially sorry for Anna- (or as she was now calling herself, Anne-) Marie. She had lost all her original family members, and her father's other children – her half-brothers and -sisters – rebuked her because she was going to give evidence against their parents. I finished off by telling the reporter that at least Fred West had paid the ultimate price for his crimes.

Then Andrew Parker from the *Sun* phoned to tell me the same news and I told him the same things that I had told the *Today* man. At that time, I didn't know any of them were going to publish my story and photos, but the next morning, 2 January 1995, there was a big centre-page spread about me in the *Sun*, along with one of my old modelling photos and all the details of what went on that night in 1972! The headline read: *I was Fred West's Sex Slave*. Thankfully, they hadn't mentioned Rose in the story, only the things that Fred had done. Obviously, they couldn't publish anything about Rose, as she still faced trial.

I was furious with them for publishing such a story without first telling me so that I would be forewarned and forearmed. I wanted an opportunity to be able to explain to my friends and family about what had really gone on. And, in particular, I was concerned that nothing should jeopardise the chance of Rose being convicted before she had faced her trial.

21

WAGGING TONGUES
HAVE EMPTY HEADS

I AGREE, NEWS coverage of such heinous crimes as those committed by the Wests needs to be reported on as a matter of public interest, but the coverage in the *Sun* newspaper, although truthful and well written, gave out a mixed signal to those who hadn't read the complete story. Some of my past friends thought I was actually dead and some wagging tongues had caused me further anguish.

After the *Sun* story appeared, it became clear that some people had obviously not bothered to read the full article through properly or were just using it as an excuse to poke fun at me. The piece deserved a full read, but local people were gossiping about me, saying that I had been Fred West's lover! The gossips thought I was admitting to being a willing participant in the Wests' sick games of lust.

One drunken young man I didn't even know to speak to

came up to me, put his arms around my waist and said, 'You're that Fred West's girlfriend, aren't you?' Ian's brother had another man come up to him in a bar and say to him, 'Good on Caroline, she shagged Fred West.'

A schoolgirl, the same age as Kelly, whom I had known all her life, was telling Kelly's classmates, 'Caroline liked sex, she only complained to the police when it got out of hand.' Kelly was too upset to say anything, but her friends did. They had a go at the girl and told me. I phoned the girl's father and told him what she had said and how, when Kelly's mates asked her why she was saying it, she said her dad had said it. I had always thought of her parents as my friends. Who needs friends like that! I had a go at him and he denied saying it, though I now know that he did. They hurt Kelly and me, but it hardened me up in readiness for what I was to face at the trial. It was gossips like him with their tittle-tattle that had stopped me pushing the rape charge in the first place – a sad person with no life of his own, so he had to take an interest in mine.

In retrospect, these chin-waggers could be held responsible for the way the Wests were allowed to continue with their killing spree, as it was the thought of the scandal that these people would spread which put me off in the first place. There are a lot of ignorant men in Cinderford and some vicious-tongued women. Wagging tongues have empty heads!

Ian was less capable of ignoring the gossip and rumours that had been going around since my story and photo had hit the headlines. He knew the truth about me so he never doubted me, but he felt angry and upset about the way I was being talked about and, as a consequence, he became almost reclusive. Now that his parents were on our side, we could have gone out together, but he didn't want to go anywhere – not where people knew us. He was afraid I would be hurt by the accusations, but I had found my fighting spirit and I knew the truth would have to have come out in the near future anyway.

In February 1995, we moved into our new house. I had asked the *Sun* for a further advance on the payment from what they still owed me so that I could completely furnish it, which they agreed to.

After Fred's death, I was informed that I was to be a witness at Rose West's trial where she now faced charges for the murder of *ten* young women. The loss of Fred West was a blow to the prosecution case and I had become a key member of their prosecution portfolio.

I was so scared. I had never expected to be called as a witness, but some bargaining had been going on between the barristers, and because the defence wanted to use Fred's taped interviews in court, in return they conceded to me being used as a 'Similar Fact' witness. In other words, what had happened to me – being bound up, the tape used to silence me and the sexual assault that took place and the threat of being kept in the cellar, then the further threat of being murdered and buried – was similar to what must have happened to the victims that were found at Cromwell Street. The victims were found with nylon rope in their tiny graves and most still had tape around their heads, in the same way that rope and tape had been used on me.

My mum had also made a statement to the police about what happened when I got home on the morning after the abduction, and how I looked and behaved. The prosecution did not ask my mum to attend the committal proceedings, but said that she would, possibly, be questioned at the full trial.

I was going to tell the world my story and I was going to be torn apart in front of everyone, including my mum, but this time I would do it. I wanted to see Rose pay for the wicked things she had done – not so much for what she had done to me, but for the poor girls that had died.

I was feeling more guilty than Rose was about their deaths. She was still firmly denying any knowledge of their murders. I could see each of their faces and knew each of their names and something about them all and that was just from reading about them in the newspapers. Rose had actually known eleven of the twelve girl victims whose remains had been discovered; four of them had certainly lived in her home.

One, eighteen-year-old Shirley Robinson, had been the lover of both Rose and Fred. One of the twelve victims was Rose's sixteen-year-old daughter, Heather, who was murdered in 1987. Another victim was her eight-year-old stepdaughter Charmaine, one of three victims who were killed prior to the Wests abducting me, in 1971. Another victim was ninteteen-year-old Lynda Gough, who had been Rose's lodger and her children's nanny, as I had been. Lynda was killed in April 1973, just three months after the Wests had been found guilty of indecent assault against me.

Rose had actually lived with these girls, yet she showed no sorrow or signs of mourning when their bodies were discovered – except for Heather. I guess she had hoped Heather would not have to die, but Heather had threatened to let their secrets out and so had to be silenced.

I looked at the faces of these girls with a great sense of sadness and guilt about their deaths. I wanted to free myself of the guilt I felt, and the only way I could do it was to tell the police exactly what Rose was capable of when she was at the beginning of her depraved career, when she had been into sexual depravation and knew that Fred had already murdered.

In my mind, she was capable of murder; after all, it was Rose, and not Fred, that had smothered me with the pillow. Had it not been for Fred removing the pillow when he did, I could have died, killed by Rose's hand.

Instead of the dismembered and mutilated body of Lynda Gough crammed into the tiny grave beneath the rear bathroom extension of the house, it could have been mine.

22

DEATH OF A MATRIARCH

ON WEDNESDAY 19 April 1995, at 10am, the answering machine clicked on and I could hear my brother Rob speaking, asking me to phone him. His voice sounded flat and I sensed that something was wrong, so I jumped out of bed and called his number.

His wife, Lynne, answered; she was crying and unable to get her words out. Then she said, 'I'm so sorry! Your mum's dead! We think she had a heart attack sometime yesterday evening.' Through her sobs, she added, 'Alison, the warden, found her fifteen minutes ago on the bedroom floor. Rob has gone down there and the others are on their way, I'm so sorry.'

I was on my own with fifteen-month-old Shannon, and six-year-old Shani-Jade. Ian was at work. Kelly had stayed the night over at her friend Hannah's. I phoned my friend, Sharon, who lived opposite Hannah, and told her through my tears, 'My mum has died, could you go over Hannah's and tell Kelly to come straight home? Please don't tell her what has happened, I'll tell her myself.'

Sharon offered to come round and look after the girls for me while I took Kelly down to Mum's bungalow.

When Kelly came home, she said, 'It's Nan, isn't it?'

I told her, 'Yes, she died sometime last night.'

We hugged and cried, then went to Mum's. Rob, Sue and Alison were there when we arrived.

Kelly went looking for her nan. Sue tried to stop her, saying it would be too upsetting for her, but Kelly pushed her aside and went to the bedroom. I followed her.

Mum was down on the floor behind the door. She was on her knees, her face to the floor.

Kelly cried, 'Oh, Nan!' as she kneeled on the floor next to my mum, and put her arms around her and kissed her. 'We have to get her up and on to the bed, we can't leave her like this!' she cried, trying to lift her nan. 'Help me, Mum!' she sobbed. It was a heartbreaking scene.

The doctor came; he said my mum had most probably died of a heart attack and that she must have been sitting on the bed and fallen forward. He said it would have been quick – she would have been dead before she hit the floor, which we all agreed was a blessing. When we used to tease her, Mum had very often told us, 'You'll be sorry when you find me dead in my bed one morning!' And she was right.

When the doctor left, I had five minutes alone with Mum. Talking softly to her and stroking her hair back off her face, I told her how much I loved her and how I wished I had told her so before. I gave her a kiss and joined my brother and sister in the lounge.

Kelly went back into the bedroom and sat with her arms around her nan. Sue and Rob were both quite calm, but I'd seen Rob like this before when he was a teenager, when Alf died. We all thought he had coped well, until the day after Alf's funeral, when we found him drunk and crying on the green in front of our house. He was crying for his dad; he wanted to die so he could be with his dad.

Mum's little bungalow soon grew crowded as my family came to say their goodbyes. My youngest sister Stacey and the twelve-year-old daughter of Angela had been with Mum the previous night. Stacey had left at 8.00pm and said Mum was fine when she left her. Mum had made herself a sandwich and was going to sit in bed and make an audiotape to send to her brother Sid. Mum and Sid had got into the habit of sending talking tapes instead of writing letters, but she hadn't started the tape and she hadn't changed into her bedclothes. The sandwich was on the bedside cabinet, with one bite taken out of it, so she must have died soon after Stacey left.

We all had five minutes on our own with Mum, to say our goodbyes. We all handled it differently. Sue and I started tidying up. Rob and Adrian wandered around trying not to cry. Rick (Richard) and Angela cried and cried. Stacey sat quietly stunned. Keith, who had never really got on with Mum, was quiet and he looked uncomfortable. I thought maybe he was feeling as I had when Alf died. I was glad that he came to see her, even though he felt he would have been a hypocrite if he attended her funeral.

We buried Mum on Thursday 27 April 1995 in with Alf at the Yew Tree Cemetery. It's a lovely cemetery on the eadge of the forest. It was Mum's choice, what she had wanted. We invited DC Morgan and DS Barbara Harrison, who had attended the service, back for refreshments.

When we got back to my place, we discovered a photographer waiting with his camera at the ready. Rob saw him off. He was angry that the photographer knew it was Mum's funeral and was showing us no respect for our feelings. I think if the photographer had argued or hung around, Rob would have ended up in the cells for the night. He needed something to take his anger out on.

We had friends and family around to celebrate Mum's life. It was a lovely sunny day so we all sat outside on the patio and had a few drinks. We all told our funniest moments that we shared with Mum who, by the way, happened to have a great sense of humour and a weak bladder – a bad combination. The times we used to hold her rocking chair back and she'd be struggling and giggling with her legs in the air! She'd be screeching at us to put her down, but we didn't put her down till she wet herself. She would run to the toilet laughing and cursing us at the same time. Her favourite curse, we used to call 'Mum's three Bs': 'You bollocking ballsing bastards,' she'd shriek.

Mum had gone deaf over the last ten years of her life and wore a hearing aid. Sometimes, when there were a few of us around her house, we would all mime or talk in whispers and she would change her batteries or turn her hearing aid up. Once it was turned up we would all talk extra loud, forcing her to tear the hearing aid out of her ear. She used to really curse us for that.

On another occasion, when Rick was staying with her (Mum was in her sixties at the time) she asked him, 'What's the big deal with this cannabis stuff then?' Mum asked if she could try some. Rick made a joint and shared it with her. Twenty minutes later, Mum was wandering around the bungalow. 'I've forgotten what I was looking for,' she said. Then she was mooching in the pantry for something to eat. 'This stuff doesn't do anything for me,' she said, as she got herself a big plate of snacks and biscuits. Rick started laughing at her, and then she started laughing and running, once more, for the bathroom!

Our mum was one of the best, always managing to cope with us all, as children and as adults; she was always there for us. As her 21 grandchildren came along, one by one, she helped with them too. Always willing to babysit, sometimes for five children at a time. She would always babysit for other young mums from the Hilldene estate too. When I was still living at home, it was nothing to find two or three babies staying over for the night, carrycots in the front room and Mum sleeping on the sofa.

In later years, she looked after her grandchildren and my friends' children. She was very close to my daughter, Kelly; there was a special bond between them. They loved each other very much. I often think if it wasn't for Mum being so openly affectionate with Kelly, when I couldn't be, Kelly wouldn't have been as confident and outgoing as she is today.

Kelly spent a lot of time with her nan, and it was through Kelly that other youngsters got to know her nan too. In the holidays or on the weekends, Kelly would very often stay at her nan's and two or three of her schoolmates would stay too. They would play cards or watch TV and eat a Chinese take-away together.

Mum was sympathetic towards the youngsters and listened to their problems and helped them out. She was an adoptive nan to many of Kelly's schoolmates. That's why twenty boys and girls from Heywood Secondary School attended her funeral. They would miss their Nanny Harris too – a great matriarch!

23

LIFE GOES ON

A WEEK AFTER Mum's funeral, I went to a spiritualist church. I know a lot of people reading this will have sought solace in this way; many scoff at such spiritual contact and believe it to be an evil kind of sorcery. All that I can say is that when you have lost a loved one, all such thoughts fall by the wayside. When you love someone, you don't let your mind rule your heart.

I felt I needed to go there for some proof that my mum was in heaven – plus, I liked the atmosphere at the Monmouth Christian Spiritualist Church. I already felt an affinity with spiritual things. The spiritualist church was a happy place and the people who went there were always really friendly, they all had a good – and sometimes naughty – sense of humour. The atmosphere wasn't stuffy like other church services I'd been to. Earlier in the year, when I was depressed about all the victims of the Wests, Sue, who had taken me there a few times earlier, had introduced me to the members of the congregation.

Most people who go to a spiritualist church for the first time go because they have lost a loved one and want reassurance that they are safe in heaven. They want to believe it, but they need proof; or they are just curious after seeing something about it on TV or hearing something about it from someone who has been to a spiritualist church before.

They want to see what it's all about and learn more about it. Many go thinking that everyone will all sit round in a circle in the dark holding hands, and the medium will bring ghosts through so that everyone can see them, but it's not like that at all. It is a place of joy where you can feel uplifted – well, it certainly was in my case.

I was ready to crack from all the things that were going on in my head. I needed to know that the girls who had been murdered were safe and happy, and I had hoped to get a message from one of them so I could be sure they were there – though as it turned out, I never got a message from them.

I enjoyed listening to the guest medium giving other people messages, bringing through the personality of the deceased and telling their loved ones things that no one would have guessed at. Things that maybe only the deceased and the person getting the message would know.

You could tell by the look on the faces of the people who got the messages that it was all true and they would sometimes shed a tear of happiness knowing their loved ones were well again and still having the same personalities they had while on earth, though maybe a little softer now and more understanding. Many who have come back say they are sorry for the way they left, especially if they had had sudden deaths such as heart attacks and accidents, and they always say they are with you and not in the graveyard.

On 25 May 1995, George Smith, a medium from Cymbran, came to me with a message. George has quite an eccentric appearance with his white wavy, collar-length hair. The way he communicates with the spirits, you can almost see them too. George is a wonderful medium and a hard-working fundraiser for charities,

I was both nervous and excited at the prospect of finding out who the message was from. Sylvia, who runs the church with her husband Derrick and friend Frank, wrote down what she could of my message and gave it to me at the end of the service.

The medium said he had a young man for me: 'He's in his twenties.' George clutched his head and said, 'This man died on impact suddenly, head injuries.' He told me lots of things about the man, who was obviously my boyfriend Gary who had died in a bike accident in October 1985. The medium told me, 'This man had a grin from ear to ear. He wore a shirt, jeans and a leather waistcoat. He is going on about his funeral; he said it was a great send-off. He had many friends on the earth plane. He said he was on his way to a celebration [my birthday] when he died and he loves you very much.'

He went on to talk about another man who had joined the first one. He described him as having dusky skin, dark hair and wearing a fringed leather waistcoat. I said I wasn't sure who it was, as I had lost so many of my male friends. Then he told me that the man has said to tell me, 'Marjorie Proops'. Immediately

I knew who it was: it was Dave Reed! He had used the password we had agreed on. Unlike Houdini, who had not been able to make contact with his wife from the other side, Dave Reed had managed to contact me! He went on to say that they were all together on the spirit plane, all friends and very excited that they had managed to get through to me.

He said, 'David is getting very emotional, he doesn't want to leave you yet, he has one more thing to say,' and added, 'My conception of what it is like here was not quite right: it's brilliant!'

I felt so happy when I went home. Ian and a friend, Tracy, had been at the church with me when I got the messages. Tracey, who had been one of our crowd since back in the eighties, knew who the messages were from too. We were all completely astounded at how accurate George Smith had been. He must truly be able to see spirits and converse with them as easily as he would any man on earth

Then, in October, when I was getting nervous about being a witness at Rose West's trial, I went to the church and received a message from my mum! Via the medium, she told me, 'The happiest times we had were when we laughed together.' She didn't tell everyone that we also both usually ended up peeing ourselves when we got laughing, thank goodness! She then told me I had something important coming up and that I just had to be honest and I would come through it really well.

The message from Mum went on to say that there was a bit of trouble to do with a financial promise and that I was not to worry about it, as 'they' would honour their promise. I took that to mean the *Sun* newspaper.

She said she would be with me and help me through it all. My stepfather, Alf, came through at a later date and said I had always been a rebel. Then he said, 'That's my girl,' which upset me, as I wished things had been that affectionate between us when he had been here on earth.

24

THE TRIAL

I WAS INFORMED that I was to attend the Rose West trial
committal proceedings at Dursley Court. In order for me to
become accustomed to surroundings, DC Jeff Morgan and DS
Barbara Harrison took me there to show me the place. I was
shown the small cell that Rose would be held in during the
proceedings and the open-door toilet she would use if the
need occurred.

Then, two days before the case was to proceed, the trial was
changed from a witness to a paper committal – which meant all
witnesses' statements were to be read out rather than the
witnesses needing to attend. The press was allowed to hear the
statements that were read out but was forbidden to publish
anything at that time.

Being a witness wasn't something that entered my mind as
something that would enhance the story that the *Sun* newspaper

was going to do on me. When the *Sun* found out that I was to be a witness, they wanted more and offered me extra money for the human-interest side of things, including photos of Ian and my girls too. The increased payment promised was double the original £10,000. It was too much money to turn down, so I agreed.

The news about me being a witness had spread fast and everybody was trying to get interviews with me or get photographs. One day I had *GMTV*, *HTV News*, *BBC News*, *Central News* and various independent documentary filmmakers sat outside my house. We had to change our phone number and go ex-directory in the end to try to regain some privacy.

In order that I would become accustomed to the layout of the highly daunting atmosphere of a crown court and get used to the proceedings during the Rose West trial, Ian and I visited Winchester Crown Court with DC Morgan and the recently promoted DS Harrison. We visited court No. 3, where the trial would be held, and then we sat in on a murder trial in one of the other courts.

A young man had killed his female boss on the way home from a works Christmas party. He was accused of strangling her. (Later, he was found guilty.) Afterwards, I wished I hadn't gone in there – it was horrible! I decided I didn't want Ian to be at the court when I gave evidence. I think he felt that he should be there to support me, but I preferred to do it on my own as he hadn't handled things very well up until then.

When I talked about the forthcoming trial, Ian hated hearing about it and he said it hurt him too much, because there was nothing he could do about it now as it had already happened before he was even born.

On Tuesday 3 October 1995, the trial of Rose West started. I followed every bit of news coverage – and there was plenty of it. Every TV station, radio station and newspaper was covering the trial. Everyone was talking about it; everywhere I looked I saw Rose West's face looking back at me. The scenes of the media cameramen lining the street to the court and chasing after the police van with its motorcycle escort that carried Rose West to and from the court was extremely intimidating.

Photographers were up trees, on walls and some were even on ladders. All were desperate to get a snap of anyone connected to the trial, especially Rose West herself. I, too, was to face the prospect of running the media gauntlet.

The barristers, Mr Brian Leveson, QC, for the prosecution and Mr Richard Ferguson, QC, for the defence, had discussed legal technicalities about what evidence the jury should hear in the coming weeks and had given their long opening speeches. I didn't know anything about these legal arguments at the time, but Richard Ferguson had argued that my evidence and the evidence of two other women who had experienced Rose's sexual deviances first hand and survived to tell the tale had no place in the trial. Brian Leveson, however, insisted that what had happened to all three of us at the hands of Rosemary West showed an established pattern of behaviour, behaviour that was repeated in the killings, and won the argument. This enabled him to apply the principle of 'similar fact evidence', which I referred to earlier.

Another thing that was to come up again and again in connection with the evidence was the fact that many witnesses, including myself, had entered into contracts with different tabloids and TV stations and it was felt by the defence that the payment of large amounts of money for our stories had, somehow, caused us to exaggerate what actually happened to us, or what we saw or heard. I can only speak for myself when I say I never exaggerated anything. I didn't need to, and I would not have even considered it, especially not for the sake of sensationalism to sell to the *Sun*. The truth in itself was sensational enough.

I gave the *Sun* the same written account of what happened to me at the hands of the Wests as I had given to the police two weeks prior to them coming on the scene. I saw nothing wrong in being paid for something that was mine, and so personally mine. At the time of selling my story, I had no idea that I would have to be a witness; if I had, things may have been different.

The Sunday before the trial commenced I felt the need to hear something positive, so I went to the spiritualist church. I received a message telling me, 'You have been trying on clothes for an important occasion that is coming up.' (I had been trying to find something suitable for my court appearance, something that looked smart but comfortable.) The message finished by saying, 'You have been worrying about things, but there is no need. If you just take your time, everything will turn out fine. You are not alone.'

I had found some comfort in the message at the time, but when the actual morning of my day in the witness box was upon me, I was not so confident. On 10 October 1995, I was up at 5.00am. DC Morgan and my newly assigned Victim Support lady, Immy, came to pick me up.

Immy, a pretty, bespectacled, fair-haired Dutch lady a few

years older than myself, was to become my confidante in the days and years to follow. That morning, very little conversation was to be had on that long nerve-wracking drive to Winchester. It was Immy's job to look after me at the court, but we were not allowed to discuss the evidence or have anything thing to do with the other witnesses with whom we would be meeting. I was worried about seeing the other witnesses, especially the lodgers. Even after 22 years, I still felt embarrassed about what had happened with them.

We met up with the other witnesses at the rendezvous police station several miles outside of Winchester, where we were to get on the minibus that would take us on to Winchester Crown Court.

We met up with DS Barbara Harrison there too; she was escorting another witness that morning. As I walked into the station, I came face to face with my past as I recognised a man walking towards me. It was one of the lodgers – Ben Stanniland! His long hair was now collar length, but the years had been good to him and he was still as handsome as I had remembered him. He recognised me too; he nodded hello to me and I nodded back, but kept on walking. With Ben was with another man, Dave Evans, who had also been a lodger at the house in the seventies. He looked vaguely familiar, but I couldn't really say that I remembered him. I was grateful for the fact that I didn't see my attacker who had tried to rape me at Cromwell Street, as I'm sure he would have made me feel like dirt, the way he had in the past. He wasn't the most pleasant of men back in the seventies and I doubted he had changed for the better over the years.

Among the witnesses were a smartly dressed silver-haired couple whom I was told were Mr and Mrs Gough, Lynda's parents. I wondered if they held me responsible for the death of their daughter. Whatever they felt, I felt responsible for Lynda's demise. I wanted to speak to them, to hug them and ask their forgiveness for being alive when their daughter was dead. Mrs Gough looked so sad and nervous. Mr Gough looked up at me, gave me a lovely warm smile and nodded hello to me. I smiled back at him, a smile that I hope said, 'I'm sorry about Lynda and I promise I will do my best to get some kind of justice for her death.'

We boarded the minibus and sat quietly for the ten-minute journey through Winchester. We could see out of the minibus windows, but the waiting press could not see in. Still, they ran chasing after us with their collective flashes, like disco strobes, bouncing off the windows. One photographer fell over and somersaulted in the road, which brought a giggle from Dave Evans, who was already halfway down his pocket-sized bottle of brandy, which he had been discreetly sipping on during the journey.

We were driven around to the back of the court to avoid the media, but as we got out of the minibus flashes were blazing all around us. There were TV crews and hundreds of photographers all over the place hiding behind walls, including one I had met from the *Sun* who had taken some family shots of Ian, Shannon, Kelly and me.

Some photographers were sat up trees snapping away; some would pop up from behind high walls, take photos and then duck down when a police officer approached. If it hadn't been such a serious occasion, I would have found it all quite funny, seeing them all jostling each other and scrambling up walls, trees and ladders to get a photo, but they only got a picture of us in the lobby, waiting for the lift. This was a picture that I would see time and time again on TV in the next week or so.

Once we were cosily tucked away inside the court waiting rooms, we sat and waited our turn to give evidence. The witnesses were split up into two waiting rooms – when you were the next in line to go into the witness box, you were separated off from the others.

I was also assigned a member of the Victim Protection Service – in my case, a very smart-looking gentleman in his fifties, called Mark. He kept all unwanted attention away from me; he would check the corridors to make sure no media were hiding when I needed the toilet. He made sure we were comfortable and fetched us drinks and food and generally kept us informed about how things were progressing. When it was my turn to go into the solo waiting room, Dave Evans offered me a swig of his brandy which I accepted, needing a little extra Dutch courage.

It was a long wait, but Immy and I talked all the time about things that had happened to me during my childhood and I discovered I wasn't odd, and that other young women were very much the same as me. I wasn't a slut, I wasn't a bad child. I was simply a child that had got up to all the same things that a lot of other children had, but I had been made to feel guilty about them all my life instead of just accepting that it was all a painful part of the growing-up phase of life. I found it easier to talk to Immy than I did to my counsellor because she gave me feedback; she didn't just listen or ask the odd question and watch the clock.

I was feeling much more confident by the time the CPS (Crown Prosecution Service) man came to go over what was happening and read through my statements. I was as ready as I would ever be to go and face Rosemary West and the world, naked and with nothing to hide.

I was feeling strong. I had twenty minutes to wait and then I would be in that courtroom, facing Rose West for the first time in more than twenty years. I had read how she had sat staring at her sister and mother when they gave their evidence the day before, so I decided I would look her in the eyes and not be the first to turn away. I thought if I could do that, I could do anything.

I was doing fine until a big fair-haired man in his fifties entered the room and sat down opposite us. He looked somehow familiar but I couldn't place him. Then he leaned forward in his seat and with a big smirk on his face he said, 'Hello, Caroline, nice to see you again after all these years.'

I stared at him in disbelief, unable to speak.

He went on, 'You don't remember me, do you?'

He was still grinning that same grin I had last seen some 22 years earlier when he had told me I was 'game for it'. When he made me think I was a slut. When he made me feel so ashamed of myself that I had no courage to face up to the Wests and have them locked away where they couldn't hurt anyone.

Finding my tongue at last, I almost whispered, 'What's your name?' Knowing damn well what his name was.

'Detective Kevin Smith,' he said, sounding as if I should be happy to see him, like a long-lost friend.

'Oh yes, I remember you now!' I screamed at him, making the CPS man who had been sitting quietly going through some papers nearly fall off his chair. Mark came rushing back into the room, followed by two police officers.

Even nasty Detective Smith jumped back in his seat, looking stunned by my outburst, before he was led away by his uniformed colleagues. My voice reverberated around the room, 'Get him out of here! Get him out of here!' I was still shouting even after they had gone and closed the door behind them.

My shock turned to anger and then to the inevitable tears. Detective Smith had no idea how much of an impression he had made on me, a negative impression that had stuck in my subconscious and added to my already low self-esteem, plummeting my self-respect to an all-time low and colouring my pathway through life with a dark shade of secrets and shame. I realised he had been ignorant back then and that nothing had changed. He still didn't understand women. He's a man's man – very insensitive.

Immy was furious about him being allowed in the same room as me. I had told her how I felt about him only hours earlier when we were talking about my feelings of shame. She waited with me in the washroom, while I tidied myself up and repaired my make-up. All my courage had gone out the door – along with Detective Smith.

I entered courtroom No. 3 through a door behind the witness box. As I was led to the box, I saw, seated to the left of me, some of the detectives I had met or been interviewed by over the previous 22 months. They all gave me a look of support.

I faced forward and scanned the many faces. Across the room, I could see and recognise members of the media, TV and press.

I noticed Andrew Parker; he was looking up at me and gave me a discreet nod of encouragement. Then, next to the press but on a higher level, I saw the jury of eight men and four women. They were all looking at me. One young man on the end of the front row gave me a little smile, which made me smile back.

Looking straight ahead, but at a lower level than the box, I could see tables where the barristers and their staff sat dressed in all their courtroom finery of robes and wigs. Mr Leveson, a shortish man with big dark eyes, gazed up at me, looking over his spectacles and gave me a polite nod with just a hint of a smile. He was on my side and he looked a much kinder person than the tall, snooty-looking Ulsterman who was Rose's team captain, Mr Richard Ferguson.

Then I looked up and to my left, and there she was: Rose West looking down on me. I thought, this is it, don't turn away and, giving her a long look and holding the stare, I noticed how old, frumpy and unfit she looked. There were only two years between our ages, but I had certainly worn better than she had, even with all the grief in my life. I held my unblinking eyes on hers until she turned away. I'd done it! I'd stared her out. That was a good start.

I looked once more at the prosecution barrister, Mr Brian Leveson; I said a prayer asking my mum to help me to be strong. Suddenly, I felt my whole body straighten up as if someone had moved into my torso, shoving my innards to the side and forcing me to stand straight and tall and proud. I looked at the two barristers and said to myself, this is a game, we are two teams in a final and we both want to win – Mr Ferguson and Rose in one team and me and Mr Leveson in the other. It is nothing personal; whatever he asks me, I will answer truthfully, however bad it might make me look, whatever dark secrets I have to disclose. I will not get upset; I will not cry or get angry. I will give my evidence as clearly and slowly as possible. I will listen and think before I answer. I will not be made to say something I didn't mean to, and as long as I am honest and tell the whole truth they can't ask for more, the rest will be up to the jury.

As Mr Justice Mantell entered the room from his chambers, I stood tall and looked him in the eye too. I remember thinking he had kind eyes; he looked like an old headmaster of mine from Bilson Infants School called Mr Williams. A nice firm but fair man, a grandfatherly type, though Mr Justice Mantell looked much grander in his scarlet robes than Mr Williams ever did.

That first day in the witness box, Brian Leveson questioned me for the prosecution. He asked me to tell what had happened to me on 6 December 1972. I told him everything that had gone on that night – all the sordid details! The whole room was silent and all eyes were on me, yet I didn't feel shy or embarrassed. I just kept talking, telling them everything I could remember. I was there to tell them all what kind of people the Wests were and what they were capable of. I looked at Rose every time I had to mention something she had done or said, to see her reaction, but she never looked back at me again. I wanted her to see that I would not let her intimidate or domineer me; she sat there looking down at her lap the whole time. I thought to myself she already knew what had happened that night so nothing I said would get a reaction from her, unlike the poor people in the gallery, who gasped, tutted or shook their heads in disbelief at what they were hearing. They were normal everyday people drawn to that court room, not knowing what would come out, shocked and sickened as they listened to me and other witnesses tell of our involvement with the evil Rose West, now in the guise of a dowdy, bespectacled housewife who sat out of sight below them. They didn't need to see her, they already knew what she looked like due to the massive media coverage prior to the trial, but looks can be deceiving. For some, it was harder to take than others, the 'others' being the families of the murder victims. I felt for them. I knew they were picturing their daughters' faces in my situation as I recounted what had happened to me.

It was their daughter that was tied up, punched and prodded and abused, their daughter who was humiliated and taunted and raped and threatened with being kept prisoner to be used and abused again and again. But it was not their daughter standing in front of them telling the tale of 25 Cromwell Street and of the horrors it had kept secret for two decades. That dire act was left to the few lucky survivors.

Their daughters had been driven deeper and deeper into the clutches of evil and then released into a better world, a world of peace and love, out of reach of the evil that they had endured. Never to be touched by evil again. That was what I was learning to believe, wanting to believe, and wanted the victims' families to believe. Going to the spiritualist church had taught me that this life is hell, and that death is the gateway to heaven, where we really come to life.

Amongst the victims' families were victims of another sort:

Rosemary's babies. I had seen Stephen West with a beautiful half-caste girl who, I later discovered, was Tara West, Rosemary's daughter by one of her Jamaican lovers. I felt for them too. They had suffered at the hands of their parents. Not to the same degree as the murdered girls, of course. Nonetheless, they had suffered greatly, either mentally or physically and in some cases both. Unlike the other people in the gallery, they felt love for their assailants. They had lost their dad, their home and now they were on the verge of losing their mother. To the average person in the gallery, Rose West looked like any other mother, neighbour, housewife, but her lifestyle and her insatiable sexual appetite was not like any of theirs. They – and the jury – must have found it hard to believe what I was saying.

The press and the police knew what was coming out. They became hardened to it at the committal proceedings at Dursley Court earlier in the year, which had reduced many of the hard-nosed pressmen and women to tears.

But the jury and the people in the gallery were not ready for the horrors that they would get to hear from me, Anne-Marie and Miss A, a young woman in her thirties who had been living in Jordons Brook House, a children's home not far from Cromwell Street, at the height of the murders. It was 22 years since it had all happened, but it was like yesterday in my mind, and I should imagine it was the same for the other two surviving victims of Rose West.

My first day in the witness box had exhausted me. I decided not to take the three-hour journey home that night and, instead, I stayed in a hotel a few miles outside of Winchester. That evening, I showered and changed from my smart black skirt suit into a pair of jeans and a jumper, took a walk to the telephone box and called Ian.

As soon as I heard his voice, I wanted to go home. I was missing him and the girls and Ian was worried about me. I told him I felt I had someone step in and take over my body and mind, someone very strong. A good spirit from heaven was helping me and I knew it, and told Ian so. He most probably thought I was cracking up with the pressure of it all, but he humoured me. He wished me luck for the next day and told me he was missing me and that he loved me. Then we said good night.

I was starving. All I had eaten all that day was a sandwich that the kindly Mark had given me at 12 o'clock, so I went into a Chinese restaurant and had a sit-down meal on my own. I felt embarrassed and self-conscious, wondering if anyone there had seen my face on the news and knew who I was. I rushed my meal, went back to the tiny room in the nice guesthouse and watched *Soldier Soldier* on the TV. I loved that programme and I hoped it would cheer me up, but I couldn't stop worrying about the next morning and having to face Rose West's barrister, Ferguson. He would be trying to make me feel bad about myself. He would call me a liar. He would tell the world about me and the lodgers. He would try to convince the world that I was as bad as Rose West when it came to sex. I was dreading it, but I knew I had to do it.

I said a prayer and asked the spirits and Mum to be there for me again in the morning, and I said to the girls who had died, 'I'll do it for you. I'm so sorry.' Then I fell asleep quietly crying as I saw each of the dead girls' faces. I will never forget any of those faces; they are with me for life.

The following morning, I woke at 6.30, showered, applied my make-up, put my long dark hair up and fixed it in place with a navy blue bow that matched my navy blue miniskirted suit. I wore black strappy high-heeled sandals. I suppose, some might say, I looked sexy, not appropriate for the courtroom, but I often wore miniskirts, usually with knee-length boots, or tight jeans and clingy T-shirts. Most of my clothes were black, except for the odd jumper and blouse. I had dressed this way since I was twenty years old, when I was into motorbikes, the men and the lifestyle that went with them. I had been a rebel most of my life, and I wanted the jury to see that in me. I didn't want them to think I was trying to con them into thinking I was a 'Goody Two Shoes'. I had been around and I wasn't going to deny it.

This time I was older and a little wiser. I didn't care what people thought of me any more; their opinions meant nothing to me. I could rise above their ideals of what I should look like or behave like. As long as I had a clear conscience, I knew I was OK.

I stood back so I could see my whole image in the wardrobe mirror. I looked smart and self-assured and, most importantly, I felt comfortable. I felt like me.

At 7.00am, DC Morgan and Immy came for me. I felt fine until I got in the car; then I began to feel heavy, like the whole world was on my shoulders.

I didn't say much on the journey to the rendezvous station. My escorts knew I was worried and kept reassuring me that I'd be fine. The more they were nice to me, the more I felt like crying, but I managed to keep calm.

At the rendezvous station, I accepted an apology from one of the detectives for being put in the same room as Detective Smith. I was told that he was in the building, but would be kept away from me. We all got in the minibus and drove through the hoards of waiting photographers.

By 10.30am, I was back in the witness box. Again, I spotted Andrew Parker from the *Sun* and gave him a little smile. He gave me a wink and a nod of support. I didn't like Andrew's tactics sometimes, but I did quite like him as a person. I knew he was concerned for me and knew that I was under a lot of pressure. Not only was I going to have to tell all my secrets, I was also going to be accused of telling lies to make more money from the *Sun* for my story.

I turned to my left and there, sat next to me in the police seats as promised, was DC Jeff Morgan. I felt better knowing he was close by. He knew all there was to know about me and he still seemed to like and even respect me.

The jury filed in and Rose took her seat, flanked by two female guards. Again, I looked over at her; she sat looking down into her lap, as she did throughout the rest of my time in the witness box.

I knew I was in for a tough time and that I was at the mercy of Rose's barrister, so I said my prayer and waited. It happened again! My body felt like someone had moved in. I stood tall and looked around at the faces in the courtroom. I knew I had to keep calm and not get upset or flustered and, when the judge walked in, I was ready.

The questions began and I answered them all honestly. Mr Ferguson was getting nowhere, scoring no points for his team. I was strong when he mentioned that I had slept with two lodgers.

'A mistake,' I said.

He was quick. 'Two mistakes,' he retorted.

'That's correct,' I replied, not at all touched by his sarcasm.

'I put it to you that you were not forced into having sex,' he said.

'I was,' I firmly replied.

'You were not raped,' he fumed.

'I was,' I replied as I stared him in the eye.

'I put it to you that you were not hit with a belt,' he said in a stern manner.

'I was,' I replied once more, with added conviction in my voice.

'You were hit six times with the buckle end of the belt, yet you did not bleed,' he said in a mocking and incredulous way before looking around at the jury for added impact.

'No,' I replied, unflustered by his smugness, then added, 'I had the weal marks, but there was no blood.'

I was shown some photographs of my injuries. They were black-and-white prints showing my back, wrists and face. The rope burns across my back, arms and wrists showed up fine, but he wanted me to point out the so-called injuries to my face.

I told him, 'I was hit in the side of the head, on the temple. The bruising would not show up on black-and-white photos.' Gaining confidence, I added, 'Why did the photographer take a picture of my face if there was nothing to see as evidence? There was bruising on my cheek, but it didn't show up well in the black-and-white photos, that's all.'

Then he moved on to the photograph of me in the centre pages of the *Sun* dated 2 January 1995 and said, 'You told the court that you were deeply upset when you heard that Fredrick West had hung himself, yet you don't look too upset in this photograph of you in the *Sun*, the day after his death!'

He passed me the paper opened at the centre pages. The headline, *I Was Fred West's Sex Slave* in bold print was placed before me, the headline that had caused me so much grief! The barrister was referring to the photo of me in leather boots, cut off leather jeans and a black-and-gold-coloured Lurex blouse. I looked full of life and happiness, as he had already pointed out.

'Can you tell me what date this photo was taken?' he asked with that smug look firmly back on his face.

I knew what he was up to. He was trying to say that when Fred West died and the *Sun* and I got together that it was at that time that the glamour shoot was done, while I was supposedly cracking up with the news that he had died.

I defeated that implication when I said, 'That photo was taken in 1985.'

Mr Ferguson turned to the jury in surprise and said, 'Can you repeat that please?'

So I said it again, louder this time so that everyone could hear me clearly, 'Yes, that photo was taken in 1985!' I went on, 'The photo was taken in 1985 when I was 29. I am now 39.'

I couldn't help noticing that he looked slightly miffed and a little silly that he had got it wrong. I felt so pleased that I had scored yet another point against him and smiled at Andrew Parker, who was siting there red-faced. The *Sun* was under scrutiny too, because they had paid for my evidence and there was a lot of fuss about chequebook journalism at the time. I was being accused of dressing up the assault to make it worth more to sell. The *Sun* was being accused of making me add things, but that was all rubbish. I didn't need to lie to shock people; the truth in my case was harrowing enough.

I told Mr Ferguson that the small inset photo of me on the spread was taken during the month of March. It was me as I was when the murder investigation was going on. The thin, haggard-looking woman was me too. The stress of it all had seemed to age me overnight.

He gave up on that and went on to read some of my 1973 diary to me.

He said, 'You hitchhiked again just after the attack. You write on one page that you "laughed your head off"!'

'Yes, I did,' I replied and I went on to explain what had happened on the day in question in more detail than the space on this page can afford.

It made the people in the courtroom giggle, including the judge. The police had kept my diary since I had started giving them interviews and I knew that it could prove to the court that I was, indeed, raped.

Mr Ferguson had tried to imply I wasn't raped, but I had written in my diary on the page dated 12 January 1973 that 'Fred and Rose West were going to court today for the rape, indecent assault and ABH on me.'

I took the opportunity of showing it to him while I had the diary back in my possession. He turned white and asked to be allowed to leave the courtroom for ten minutes to go through my diary. When he returned, he said he had no further questions and had finished with the witness. I felt so relieved that it was over! I gave a big sigh and looked over at DC Morgan and smiled. He looked really happy for me and winked at me.

The judge asked if Mr Leveson had finished with his witness and he said, 'There is just one more matter I would like to clear up.'

Mr Leveson spoke to me again; I had thought it was all over. He asked if I had gone into court to make money. I thought that even he doubted me now and I felt betrayed for a second. I frowned, as I said, 'No!'

He asked, 'Then why are you here, Mrs Owens?'

I felt myself shake as a lump grew in my throat and tears were brimming. All my strength had sapped away in an instant and I broke down and blurted out, 'I came here to get justice for the girls that didn't make it, 'cause I feel it was my fault!'

'That is all, Mrs Owens, thank you.'

I was so angry with myself for crying. I had been so strong for the two days I had spent in the witness box. I had won the game with the defence team and then my own captain fouled me and brought me down. It didn't make sense at the time, but now I understand.

The next day, my final words in that witness box were to be spread over the front pages of nearly every newspaper in Britain. So was the fact that I had slept with four different men while I lived at number 25 Cromwell Street. But I didn't care.

25

LIVING VICTIMS

I WAS SO emphatically relieved that my ordeal in the witness box was over. I had hugs all around from Immy, Jeff and the witness service people, all congratulating me on my bravery and saying how well I had done.

DC Jeff Morgan said that the stress that was etched into my face just dissolved away. (We are still friends and we phone each other every now and then; Jeff has retired from the police and now works for the coroner's office in Cheltenham.) I was happy it was over and I had done my bit to help put Rose West away for the rest of her life.

We were sneaked out of court and I went home to my family, but only for a short while. We knew the media would be around now that I had given my evidence, so Ian and I went to Weston-Super-Mare for the weekend for some peace and quiet.

With the stress gone from my face, I felt and looked a lot

better than I had over those previous 22 months. I felt sorry for all the witnesses who had, in one way or another, been touched by the prevalent evil of the Wests.

Workmates of Fred's, who had listened to his wild stories bragging about what he had done to young women, stories so far-fetched and so disgusting, never dreamed they could be true. Now that they knew the stories were true, they found it hard to deal with.

One thing many of the witnesses had in common was the enormous feeling of guilt they felt for not saying something at the time. I understood that feeling of guilt only too well. It seemed that the only people who didn't feel guilt were the very ones who had committed the crimes: Fred and Rose.

One witness with whom I felt empathy was Miss A. The Wests had known many young girls from Jordons Brook House children's home and had encouraged them to call around to the house where they would make them feel wanted and lull them into a false sense of security, then sexually abuse them. One of these girls was Miss A, at that time a fifteen-year-old girl. She told the court how she had come to look on Rose as a surrogate older sister, whose shoulder she could cry on. One day, when she called around to see Rose, that had all changed. Rose led her to a bedroom where another girl of around fifteen years old was lying naked on a bed. (Anne-Marie thought it might have been her.) Miss A told the court how she was raped and buggered by Fred and sexually assaulted by Rose, who used dildos on her, amongst other phallic-type objects. She went on to tell the court that she had witnessed the other girl in the room being raped too.

Miss A had only returned to the house once more and that was at night under the cover of darkness, with a can of paraffin and a box of matches! The plan was to burn the house down with Fred and Rose in it, but when it came to carrying out the act of arson, she couldn't go through with it.

She had since spent some time as a psychiatric patient and had undergone a course of electro-convulsive therapy because she hallucinated and heard voices in her head. Mr Ferguson used these facts to undermine her reliability as a witness – that and the fact that she had signed a contract with a newspaper for £30,000 before ever contacting the police. This, I believe, didn't help to convince the public – or, I suspect, some members of the jury – that her evidence was reliable. Nowadays, she would be accused of suffering from 'false memory syndrome', but I can assure everyone that what she told the court fitted in with the way the Wests carried on.

Another witness, Arthur John Dobbs, who had been one of Rose's regular paying customers for sex, had met Rose through a contact magazine he had bought from a sex shop. He told the court how Rose had told him that Fred was having sex with the children. He further claimed that he had phoned social services anonymously sometime between 1986 and 1988 to tell them about Fred. What happened to Mr Dobbs's complaint to social services? Why wasn't it acted upon?

Other witnesses told of how they had heard screams and groaning while they had lived at the Wests' house, but had not done anything about it and how they most bitterly regretted their inaction, knowing what they knew now. Those screams will haunt them for the rest of their days.

One witness I felt should have known better than to lie to the court was Fred West's 'appropriate adult', Janet Leach. Janet had sat with Fred during his police interviews and kept him company. Fred appeared to have liked and trusted Janet. Since Rose had spurned him at their last joint appearance at Gloucestershire Magistrates' Court, Fred had come to enjoy Janet's company and he began to confide in her. Fred, it seems, told Janet a lot about his crimes and those others who were involved.

Janet Leach collapsed in the witness box and spent a weekend in hospital that caused the trial to be delayed for six days until she recovered. Once well enough to continue, she was wheeled into court in a wheelchair and a doctor was on standby right by her side.

In court, Janet had committed perjury. When questioned by Mr Ferguson about money she had been promised for a book deal, she denied ever having made any such deal, rumoured to be worth £100,000. When subsequently accused of lying, however, she merely said, 'Sorry about that.' Simple as that!

I was so disappointed in Janet. In fact, I was extremely angry with her. I was worried that Rose would get off, and chequebook journalism would be held to account, also making my evidence unreliable. The background was that a deal had been done with a national newspaper whereby Janet Leach's lover, Brian Jones, was paid the money directly so that it didn't appear as though Janet had been paid anything. This added to the courtroom drama when Janet was questioned over chalet accommodation being provided for herself, her lover and her three children. I felt it was unfair that the victims and witnesses were criticised for making money from their stories because of their knowledge of Fred and Rose, but that it was OK for the Wests' friends, family and neighbours too.

On Thursday 16 November 1995, I arranged with Immy to go to Winchester. I wanted to hear the judge's summing up of my evidence. At the last minute, DC Jeff Morgan was given permission to escort us. Not wanting to be noticed, I went disguised as a student: hair tied in plaits, spectacles (which I didn't wear back then), a woolly hat, hooded jacket, jeans and Doctor Marten boots.

We sat in the public gallery with everyone else, including the victims' families and some of the Wests' children. I sat behind Anne-Marie Davis (née West); her estranged siblings sat at the opposite end of the public gallery. Sitting on one side of Anne-Marie was Stephen and Tara West. Tara's partner sat on the other side, immediately in front of me. Two detectives sat with Anne-Marie, looking after her. Since her father's death, she had made two suicide attempts, her brothers and sisters had disowned her and they had left her out of the funeral service. Somehow, however, Anne-Marie had stolen her father's ashes from Stephen. They were all angry at each other.

I heard evidence from other witnesses in the judge's summing-up. I felt sick when he talked about little Charmaine West and stated that it was possible Rose had murdered the little girl on her own while Fred was serving a sentence at Leyhill open prison, in Birmingham for petty theft.

We went for lunch and, before returning to the courtroom, I was told that Mr Leveson wanted to see me. I waited in a small waiting room for him, feeling pretty nervous. He came in along with Detective Chief Superintendent John Bennett and they both shook my hand and thanked me for giving my evidence so articulately.

Mr Leveson said, 'I thought we got along really well, didn't you?'

I told him I had been shocked when he had asked me if I was there for the money. I told him that he had upset me a great deal with that.

'I got the reaction I needed from you,' he replied. 'It showed why you were really in court.'

I understood then why he needed to upset me: it was because I had been too strong. I had wondered if I might have come across as too controlled, too cold or even cocky. All I wanted was to get it all out, without the tears and mumbling, I wanted them to hear every word.

We returned to the courtroom and the judge recalled Anne-Marie's evidence; it was a lot worse than I had imagined! Anne-Marie sat with her head down, quietly crying. Every now and then I could see her shoulders jerking up and down as she listened to all the things she had been put through by her father and stepmother.

It had started when she was eight years old, when she had been taken down into the cellar and stripped and made to lie on a mattress on the floor. Rose had penetrated her with some kind of phallic implement while Fred held her down. She was subjected to a horrific catalogue of torturous sexual abuse by Rose and raped by her father.

That was the start of years of abuse. She was to suffer more of the same, both at the hands of her parents and at the hands of their friends, the elusive sex circle, which had, allegedly, consisted of Fred's brother John and several other men.

The abuse went on into Anne-Marie's late teens. She had even been made pregnant by her father at the age of fifteen, but had miscarried his child. The Wests had let other men have sex with her too and had also forced her into prostitution.

I found it hard to control my emotions as I listened and realised I could have saved her from all those years of suffering. I wanted to reach out to her and tell her how sorry I was and try to comfort her, but I didn't. I felt I had let her down badly and she had every right to reject my offer of an apology. I decided that one day I would write and tell her how really sorry I was.

I listened intently to what the judge had to say about my evidence, and me, and I was certain he believed every word I had said.

I left the court feeling sure that Rose West would never walk free again. That thought made me happy. Seeing how traumatised Anne-Marie was made me feel sad though. Very sad.

26

THE VERDICT

ON SUNDAY 19 OCTOBER 1995, I went to Monmouth
Christian Spiritualist Church. The guest medium came to me
with a message, which was to prove very accurate. He said,
'Something is in suspension at the moment, but once the
decision is made you will be snowballed over. You will be busy,
all at once, for a week.'

The next day at the trial, the jury retired to make their
decision. At the end of the day they adjourned for the night, as
no verdicts had been returned. I could hardly sleep that night; I
prayed that they would find Rose guilty.

On Tuesday 21 October 1995, I had kept busy around the
house all day. I had to stick close to the phone, awaiting news of
the verdict.

Immy and DC Jeff Morgan rang me in the morning to wish
me luck and let me know they were there if I needed them.

Andrew Parker rang to say he had a female reporter staying nearby who would be coming over to sit with me and take care of any reporters that might be hanging around.

Ian had got half a day off work to be with me.

My friend Karen had called in for coffee and to offer some moral support.

At 3.15pm, my sister-in-law Lynne rang and gave me the best news ever. She yelled down the phone, 'I've just seen *Sky News*. She's been found guilty of three of the murders. Congratulations!'

I couldn't control my elation, nor did I want to. I jumped up and down on the spot, screaming, 'Yes! Yes! Yes!'

Karen nearly choked on her coffee as I dragged her off her chair and spun her around the dining room. I was so happy, so relieved! I couldn't stop laughing, then crying. Karen and I raced for the kitchen roll, giggling at ourselves as the tears streamed down our faces. Ian gave me a big hug, which just made me cry even more.

Within minutes, the phone was ringing again. Immy, Jeff Morgan and Andrew Parker were all ringing to tell me the good news and congratulate me. Then family and friends were ringing. I invited them all around for a party. By 10.00pm, I was aching all over and went to bed. I slept well for the first time in months.

On Wednesday 22 November 1995, Rose West was found guilty of all ten murders. Jo Bale from the *Sun* came round at 11.00am to deal with the many phone calls from TV, radio and newspapers, passing the phone to me when friends or family called to congratulate me once again.

Friends and family came round with bottles of bubbly to

celebrate. I did an interview to round off the verdict, which had been previously arranged with Martin Brunt of *Sky News*, but his arrival was delayed, so by the time he arrived I was fairly drunk! We did the interview in my lounge; Martin was the perfect gentleman and presented me with a bottle of wine to celebrate. I felt comfortable talking to him, as he wasn't digging for the salacious details that I was trying to keep under wraps in order to protect my embarrassment.

I did the interview, which should have been a solemn affair, but I was on such a high, I had to keep stopping 'cause I couldn't wipe the smile off my face. I was just so happy that it was finally over.

27

AFTERSHOCK

CHRISTMAS 1995 SHOULD have been a happy time. Rose West was starting ten life sentences with no prospect of ever being released, Fred West had gone to hell, I had got my life back and the media circus had moved on to the next big scoop. All seemed well. But was it? My life had not been my own for nearly two years and now that I had it back it had all changed.

The outside world had been, in the most, kind and understanding towards me. Many people had said how brave they thought I was for facing up to Rose West. Yet here in my hometown of Cinderford, there were some people who had known me most of my life that were the complete opposite. Small-minded, jealous people, who had never done anything for anyone else; people who had their secrets intact; hypocrites and bigots.

One night, Ian and I went to a nearby pub for a quick drink.

It wasn't a pub we had ever been to together before, but I knew most of the people in the bar. As we walked in, everyone wanted to congratulate me and talk to me and I was overwhelmed by the response.

I left Ian to go to the bar while I renewed old friendships. When I finally got to the bar, I saw that Ian had ordered us a short each and that he had drunk his up already. Standing next to him at the bar was a married couple that I knew, Linda and Larry. I had known them since I was a little girl. I had lived with both of their families for a couple of weeks each while Mum had been in a convalescence home when I was thirteen years old. Mum hadn't wanted to leave me at home alone with Alf and the home help, whom we knew as Nanny Bishop. Mum knew I would be picked on and probably beaten without her being there to calm things down, so the neighbours offered to take me in.

I stayed with Linda's family for the first two weeks and Larry's for the next two weeks. We became good friends and I developed a crush on him, but nothing ever happened between us. His father was always nice to me, but he gave me the creeps! He was a small, ugly, grimy-looking man.

One night, I heard Larry taking a beating that his dad was giving him with a belt; it was pitiful to hear Larry begging him to stop. I couldn't take it any more and barged into the bedroom and yelled at his dad, 'Stop!'

He stopped immediately! I decided to go back home and try and behave myself. Alf and I didn't get on, but I felt I was safer with him.

So that was the background to my relationship with Larry. As

I stood at the bar next to Ian, Larry, who was drunk, sidled up to me, put his arm around me and announced to his wife, 'This was my first girlfriend.'

I didn't hear what Linda said after Larry had finished making a fuss of me, but Ian did. I glanced at him and got a shock – why was he giving me a strange, angry look?

'Drink up,' Ian said, 'We're going.'

I knew by the look on Ian's face that something was wrong, so I did as he asked. As we walked out of the pub, Linda came after me and said, 'Oh, don't go, stay and have a drink with us.' Ian grabbed my arm and pushed me out on to the pavement.

Linda was calling to me, 'Why don't you come back to our place for supper?'

Ian gave her a filthy look and said, 'No thanks, we have to go home.'

I didn't know what was going on. I thought maybe Ian didn't like the fact that Larry was all over me. As we walked the three hundred yards home, Ian said, 'That's the last time we ever go in that pub or anywhere else in this shit-hole town!' Then he went on to tell me that while I was talking to some old friends he overheard a man at the bar say, 'Here comes Caroline Raine, £70,000 the richer.' Ian also told me that after Larry had stopped fussing over me and had gone back to Linda, he had overheard Linda say to Larry, 'You never told me that you had been out with Caroline!' Then she added, 'Well, at least I never slept with Fred West!'

Ian was really upset and angry. He went on and on about how he hated Cinderford people and their jealous, nasty minds. I tried to calm him down. I told him that not all Cinderford people are like that, just the odd few, and advised not to let it get to him. I told Ian to try and ignore such people and others like them. They were all jealous of the money I'd made from the papers and all were ignorant of the fact that I had been raped or that I had suffered in any way. That day, I realised that I had been so wrapped up in what was going on with the police, the trial and the media that I hadn't noticed how badly it had affected Ian. It had been me, me and me!

When Fred West hanged himself and the *Sun* published my story, the local free paper, the *Review*, published an article in the anonymous gossip page saying they could not muster up any sympathy for me. The letter went on to say that since I had sold the sordid details of my story to the gutter press for cash, I deserved what I got. This ridiculous claim was a slur on what they called 'the gutter press', as at least the *Sun* had never said I deserved what I got and they had worked to get the story right.

Now *that* had got to me at the time! I became very angry and decided to go to the *Review*'s office and confront the editor. I was sick of everyone connecting my name to money as if I had gone out to deliberately pedal the sordid details of my ordeal at the hands of the Wests to make money.

My sister Sue, who had always been stronger than me, just wanted to barge in and punch the editor on the nose, but I didn't want that. I wanted to get my point across, give him my side of the story and give him something to think about.

I arranged to meet the editor, John Powell, two days later. I think he was expecting a load of verbal abuse from me. Instead, I sat down face to face with him and calmly told him how the media had hunted me down and how I had to give my side of the story as, otherwise, the *Sun* would have printed something in the *I Was Fred West's Sex Slave* feature that I hadn't agreed on.

I told him how hard it had been for me to have to bring it all back up again after spending 22 years trying to forget it all.

I explained how my relationship with Ian had changed, how I couldn't bear for him to touch me any more because now sex was dirty again to me.

I put it to him that I had sacrificed my privacy in order to help the police with their inquiry and how it hurt to keep seeing my name and the word 'money' mentioned in the same sentence.

Then I asked him a question. 'Have you got a daughter?'

'Yes,' he replied.

I asked, 'How old is she?'

'Sixteen,' he answered.

I asked, 'If I were to give you £1 million, would you have let her gone through what I went through with the Wests?'

'No, definitely not,' he replied, lowering his head.

'So, can you understand how it doesn't matter how much money I've been paid for my story? I would have much rather not have gone through what happened to me and remained penniless. No amount of money would compensate me for the long-term damage that has been done to me and for the feelings I have inside me now.'

I told him that I had wanted to stop the Wests getting away with murder. I didn't want any other young girl to suffer at their hands ever again, which is why I went to the police. Not for fame or fortune, but to get justice for all of those who had suffered and died at their hands. And to protect girls like his sixteen-year-old daughter, so that she might never know what it felt like to be a victim of the Wests.

After I had finished, he hung his head in shame and apologised to me.

That was the first time I had defended my actions and myself and I felt it was a turning point in my life. My self-esteem took an upward turn and I was getting stronger.

The article in the *Review* did have a positive side to it. Several young women came up to me and told me how upset they were by the article. They even went on to tell me about their own experiences of rape and sexual abuse. They hadn't told anyone about these experiences before, but now they felt they had someone to tell, someone who would understand and believe them.

One of these young women had been sexually abused by her uncle from the age of five up to the age of fifteen and she had no one to turn to. He had made her feel as though she was the one who encouraged it. Another, her foster father, had been sexually abusing her for years. He told her if she told anybody he would have her put back into the children's home – and she had been raped repeatedly by one of the boys there.

Another told me how she had been 'date raped'. Friends of the family or brothers had touched others. One victim's brother had held her down while his friends raped her. Her brother was only twelve years old at the time and she had been just ten years old.

They all had one thing in common: they all felt it was their own fault. All had gone on to sleep around or had settled for abusive relationships, thinking they didn't deserve anything better. I realised that I was not the only one who had suffered with the feeling of guilt for something I was not responsible for.

At the end of January 1996, Ian and I were going through a bad patch. He still didn't want to go out anywhere with me. He was happy to hide away indoors. I assumed it was because he was ashamed of me. I asked him to go abroad with me to try to fix our relationship, but he wouldn't leave the kids, so I took Kelly to Gran Canaria for a fortnight while Ian and Shannon were snowed in at home. When I was abroad, I celebrated Kelly's sixteenth birthday. I only had Shannon at home with Ian and Shani-Jade was with her dad.

I felt so much happier being in a different place where no one knew me, and the sunshine seemed to recharge my batteries. Although I missed the kids, I was in no hurry to return home. I would phone home most evenings to let Ian know what I was up to and to speak to Shannon.

After the first week, Ian's phone calls became very emotional. He told me that he wanted me to come back home early. When I refused, he said he never wanted me to go away without him again and then he proposed to me. I wasn't sure it was what I wanted, but he was very insistent so I said, 'Yes', thinking I'd sort it out when I got home. But when I called him again the next day, he told me he had booked it all up. He had told all our friends and family and they were very happy about it. But I was not happy about it! I felt trapped; the words 'emotional blackmail' sprang to mind.

During the second week of my holiday, I had had several nightmares about some of the Wests' victims. I could see them, bound and taped up. Tied to a chair, moaning from under their gags, pleading with their eyes – terrified eyes that were begging me to help them. Once, I lay in my bed frozen with fear. I was sure I had seen Fred West out of the corner of my eye. He was standing in the doorway to my bedroom, staring at me. It was horrible! Maybe it was my subconscious playing tricks on me because I felt I was being trapped into something I didn't really want ... yet again.

I arrived home looking tanned and healthy, but no longer feeling relaxed. The nightmares and the thought of having to talk Ian out of getting married had left me in an anxious state. I wasn't sure I wanted to marry him. For a start, he was half my age, and before long that would become a problem. I imagined he would run off with someone his own age or younger, and the thought didn't really bother me. Not really the right attitude to be entering into a marriage with.

Ian's family were happy that we were getting married, but when Ian told me weeks after my return from abroad that his mum had told him that he had no legal rights as a father if we were never married, I became furious. I got it into my head that this was the main reason he had proposed to me. It wasn't me he wanted, he just didn't want to lose his daughter. Of course, he denied it but I couldn't stop thinking it.

He had told everyone we were getting married and I felt like a fool. For the second time I was going to get married to please someone else.

Two weeks before the wedding, I discovered I was seven

weeks' pregnant. It was a bit of a shock at first, but we were pleased. I saw it as an omen; I decided I was meant to be with Ian after all.

On a beautiful hot summer's day, 15 June 1996, just perfect for a wedding, we were married at Cinderford Registry Office. Everyone was happy, including me. I wore an ivory raw silk Edwardian wedding dress and head-dress, which Ian had chosen. Our bridesmaids were Shani-Jade and Shannon, and they looked beautiful in their Bo Peep dresses. A photographer from the *Sun* came along to take photos for publication on the Monday.

DC Jeff Morgan and his wife Sal and DS Barbara Harrison, who was promoted from the rank of DC to DS after the trial, came to the wedding. I wanted them there because I had grown pretty close to them over the previous year. They had been so kind and understanding and they knew me better than most people whom I had known all my life. I had confided to them things that I had not been able to talk about for 23 years. I admired and respected them and trusted them.

Ian and I honeymooned in Devon, preferring to rent a quiet farmhouse as opposed to staying in a seaside hotel. When we returned home, I went to the spiritualist church and received a message from Mum and Alf saying, 'Fools rush in!' The message went on to say that they would be with me whatever I decided to do, that a boy child was on his way to earth, that they would be watching over him and that he would have a bronchial condition but would be OK.

On 2 February 1997, I gave birth, after a long labour, to my son, whom we named Liam David. 'Liam' for the Irish connection and 'David' after my friend David Reed and Ian's uncle Dave, who had managed to get Ian's parents to accept me into the family.

When Liam was three weeks old, he had a bad cough and we discovered he had a mild bronchial complaint, so the spirits had been right.

28

THE DUCHESS OF YORK

WHEN LIAM WAS one month old, I took him to the spiritualist church. I hoped he would feel the love and benefit from the healing in the room that I had always felt. I saw the medium who had told me Liam was coming and told her that he had the bronchial complaint that she had told me he would have. We got chatting and she told me her name was Debbie.

Debbie was a lovely young lady in her late twenties, petite, almost fragile looking, like a china doll with her black shiny hair and huge dark blue eyes. She spoke in a soft voice, with a slight London accent, and when she spoke she put everyone at ease.

I took my friend Julie with me on my first visit to Debbie's home in Monmouth. That day, as she welcomed us into her home, Debbie said, 'There is a motorcyclist and his bike waiting in here for one of you,' as she pointed into her living room. I looked, but I couldn't see anything, though I felt Gary was there.

I could smell him and the leather waistcoat he used to wear. I felt an atmosphere in the room, a lovely warm feeling. It felt like the sun had just burst through the clouds and all the light and warmth was pouring over me; it was a wonderful feeling.

Debbie didn't know about Gary, but she said, 'His name's Gary.'

That was the first time Gary came through when Debbie and I were together. Over the next year, he was to visit many more times. He told us what had been the cause of his accident: a badger had run out in front of his motorbike, he had slammed on the brakes, the chain had snapped and wrapped around the back wheel, stopping him instantly and throwing him off the bike. He said he was happy for me to be with Ian, and told me to lighten up on him. That made me realise that I could be being unreasonable about Ian and that he was doing his best; after all, he was only young. I made a mental note to be more patient and considerate of Ian's feelings.

I started go to church as often as I could, then around to see Debbie at her home. I read up on healing and mediumship and joined a 'development circle', trying to develop my psychic sensitivity so as to enable me to communicate with those that have passed on to the new life.

I was learning to be more understanding of others, and starting to comprehend how our thoughts cause things to happen, both good and bad. I wanted to be able to help others and I wanted to be able to forgive. I wanted to learn how to express love without feeling the fear of being rejected – one thing I still had to struggle with. I wanted to improve myself physically, emotionally and mentally. I didn't want to feel jealous or suspicious any more. I didn't want to keep asking Ian where he was and who he was with. I didn't want to worry if he was late home.

All my life, jealousy had driven me mad. It had cost me my happiness and – I imagined – it had physically and mentally scarred some of my boyfriends for a long time. And it had humiliated me.

I wanted to be happy and content with my life, but I also wanted to strive on and do something worthwhile. I wanted to help others, but I was too afraid to offer that help in case I let them down or they rejected my offer.

I still wasn't confident enough, but I wanted to succeed in something and decided to write a book about my life, with all the ups and downs.

The way I saw it, before I found spiritualism and since, it would be a good therapy for me, and, if it was good enough to publish, it may then help someone else who thought they were having a bad time and show them how, with some positive thoughts, it could all change.

I was learning all these things that made sense, and Ian and I started getting on better. I didn't question him about anything; I didn't feel jealous or suspicious of him any more. I felt so free. At first it worried Ian! He thought I didn't care any more, but I did. I suppose I thought, if I don't worry about him having affairs, he won't have any! Positive thinking!

I got a job back at the Xerox company in nearby Mitcheldean, on the twilight shift. It was nice to earn a decent wage again and mix with adults. And one night, my mum's spirit came to work too. Her favourite song, 'Please Release Me' by Englebert Humperdink, came on the radio and her favourite perfume filled the air. My colleagues were spooked. When the record finished, the perfume vanished too.

I was invited on to many television shows to talk about the Wests: *The Vanessa Show*, *Kilroy*, *Esther*, a religious programme called *Sunday Night* and *This Morning* with Richard and Judy. I even stood up for myself on *Westminster Live*, a political programme which that week was discussing chequebook journalism. I wasn't nervous of these TV appearances any more. All of the people I saw, I met as equals. I had learned that we were all part of one 'Great Spirit'.

One day I was with Debbie and we were just having a coffee and chatting when she started getting messages from her spirit. One of the things that were said was the name 'Fergie, Duchess of York'.

Debbie said, 'You're going to meet Fergie!'

I laughed and told her not to be so daft. I suggested that it was most probably just symbolic. Maybe the spirits meant I would be visiting York, perhaps a TV programme, as previously we had been talking about the television work I had been doing.

I didn't take too much notice, as I was more interested in the messages I was getting to do with my Irish connection. I didn't know any of them and was thinking of asking a nun who had befriended me, Sister Jude of the Carmelite Convent in Darlington, if she could help me find out more. I knew I had a brother and sister, but as far as I knew they didn't know about me, nor did their mother, and I didn't want to just show up and shock them. I had no idea if Michael, my dad, was still alive and I had been thinking about them all the time recently.

A month later, I received a telephone call asking me to appear on a new chat show for Sky TV called *Surviving Life*. I thought to myself, this will be my chance to talk about how spiritualism had helped me cope with life and improved it.

After I had agreed to do the programme, Marissa, the producer, told me the Duchess of York, Fergie, would be interviewing me. Once again, the spirits had got it right. I thought to myself, I am so lucky, not only do I get the chance to meet a woman I admired for her sense of fun – Sarah – but I get to spread the word about how my newfound faith has helped me overcome my black outlook on life.

I got straight on the phone to Debbie and gushed, 'You were right! I am going to meet Fergie.'

From then on I never doubted anything the spirits told me. Ian went to London with me to meet the Duchess of York. He had never wanted to go with me before to any of the other TV programmes I had been on, but he enjoyed it and found himself shaking Sarah's hand and liking her as much as I did.

I got on well with Sarah; we seemed to have the same sense of humour. In between shooting the hour-long programme, we talked about our children and about the fact that we were both writing our books about our lives and we promised to send each other a copy of our finished work.

I asked her if I could take a photo of her for my album. Not only did she consent to that, but also she wanted it to be a photo of us together. She got a member of the film crew to take the photo and insisted we take a couple in case one didn't come out. My camera played up and, in between shots, Sarah started fooling about pretending to kiss me. I laughed and said, 'Oh, you don't want to be doing that, the press might get hold of it, and I can just see the headlines now, "Duchess And West Victim Are Lesbian Lovers".' We both laughed at the thought of it, but knew from experience that it could happen.

I gave Sarah my address so she could send me a copy of her book, which she did and it was signed with a lovely message.

Sadly, just days after our meeting, Sarah's mother was killed in a car accident. I sent a condolences card, as many hundreds of people must have done, and I got a reply to that too. In fact, I was expecting that letter from Sarah. Debbie had told me, 'Sarah is very down, she will be writing to you soon.' Five days later, I got a 'thank you' letter from Sarah.

29

EPISTEMOLOGICAL MESSAGES

SPIRITS ALWAYS GIVE the correct message; it is the medium who sometimes doesn't translate the message correctly that confuses it. Messages come in many forms, but to receive a message from the other side constitutes something that is very sacred. The vessel that the message comes in isn't tangible, therefore it is perceived to be out of the ordinary – just because it didn't arrive in the form of a letter!

Stargazers spend endless amounts of time gazing out at what looks like nothing, yet they are able to log electrical activity and movement from many light years away, and everything that they tell us is believed to be true. So why should it be any different to a message being received from the other side?

The soul, or essence of mankind, cannot just disappear once the living vessel has perished; you can switch a light bulb off, but the electrical force that powers it is still there. By switching the switch to the 'on' position you managed to make a connection, you are the medium that has made the link possible – the telephonist at the exchange making a connection. When the light comes on, we take it for granted that someone or something must have made that happen. When a message is received from the other side then this has been made to happen by a conscious effort on the part of the medium or something that has made that connection possible. The proof of the connection is the message, which some people do not take for granted.

There are always cynical people with closed minds; I do not wish to change their opinions. There are atheists, agnostics and believers out there with regard to the spiritualist world as well as traditional religions. I am not a preacher or an advocate of telling people to see the light, for that must happen from within the person. I can only recount my own experiences and then leave it for you to decide what you make of it.

Many of the messages that come through are a mixed bundle and sometimes, at face value, they just don't make any sense. But! There are times, after careful studying, that the message is correctly interpreted and what was meant by the enciphered message becomes apparent.

A case in point occurred on one occasion when I was at Debbie's house. I had lots of messages made up of names and places that I didn't recognise. I wrote down what I could as Debbie relayed the words and messages. I have decided to share some of these epistemological messages with you, the reader.

'JEANETTE' – Spirit said, 'Jeanette Tate was one of Fred West's victims.' (Jeanette vanished while riding down a country lane in Devon on her bicycle, back in the sixties. Only her bike was found in the lane.) Spirit says there was a witness, 'Farmer Jack', but he did not come forward.

'MAN FOUND HUNG IN A BARN' – Fred had befriended fifteen-year-old Robin Holt at Sandhurst Lane caravan site in September 1966 and had taken him driving around the countryside with him in his sewage lorry.

In March 1967, Robin Holt's body was found hanging in a disused cowshed (barn) not far from Sandhurst Lane. Pornographic magazines were found beside his body.

Someone had drawn nooses around the necks of the women in the pictures. (Robin came through to another medium while I was visiting her, and told her that he was made to take part in a sexual assault and to watch what happened to the girls. He was also sexually assaulted too. He could not cope with what he had witnessed.)

'LORRY DRIVER – STATION-WAGONS – COACHES' – Job links with Fred West.

'SONG: HEAVEN MUST BE MISSING AN ANGEL' – Fred called Anna McFall his 'angel'.

'MARY' – Mary Bastholme, aged fifteen, is believed to have been a victim of Fred West's. She vanished on 6 January 1968. She had known Fred West.

What came next from Spirit left us very upset:

'HANDCUFFS ON'

'HIT IN THE MOUTH'

'TIED WITH NOOSE AROUND THE NECK, WHITE MATERIAL'

'SOMETHING WRONG WITH HER FEET'

'FINGERNAILS PULLED'
'WHIPPED'

I asked Debbie if her own thoughts could be coming through from her subconscious, possibly prompted by something that she had read about the case. She said she hadn't read or watched anything about the Wests' case after the first bodies were discovered because she was too sensitive to it all.

(Debbie had premonitions of deaths now and then, including that of three-year-old James Bulger's murder. She knew it was going to happen three weeks before it happened, but didn't know the name of the little boy or see his murderers. She only knew that a little boy was going to be led away from his mum in a shopping centre and be killed in the way that James had. It had upset her greatly and she felt unable to do anything to prevent it happening.)

The messages still kept coming over my next few visits to Debbie. I researched all the names and places using the phone book and some books written about the Wests.

'PETER' – Mary's brother was called Peter.

'ELMS/ELMSWOOD ESTATE' – Peter Bastholme's address is Elmsmere Close.

'TIM' – Mary's boyfriend was called Tim Merret, his address was Elmsgrove. (It was while Mary was waiting for a bus to visit Tim that she vanished. She had a carrier bag containing a Monopoly game with her. In 1994, a man came forward saying that he had seen Monopoly money near some recently disturbed soil in a wood at Flaxley, in the Forest of Dean, at around the time that Mary had disappeared, but he could not remember exactly where, so the police did not search the area.)

THE ONE THAT GOT AWAY

'FLAXLEY ABBEY' – Flaxley Abbey is in the area where the man saw the Monopoly money.

'BIG WATER WHEEL' – There is an old mill in Flaxley and across the road from it is a house that used to have a mill wheel.

'DARK TREE-LINED PATH' – Opposite the house is a track through the Forest. I met a man who lived in the Flaxley area in the sixties and seventies who could remember the exact spot that had been dug up, but that had been back in 1975. He said he had regularly ridden his horse up the track and one day he saw that a 4ft-deep hole had been dug and left open. The next day it had been filled in. He took me to the site. I returned to Debbie who said there was some kind of tape around one of the trees. She also had these words come through:

'HECTOR'S HOUSE' 'RED VOLVO'

I returned to the site and waited on the edge of the forest for some friends of mine to arrive. While waiting, a red Volvo estate car drove past me and on round the dirt track, which led to boarding kennels.

I recalled a TV programme from my childhood called *Hector's House*. Hector was a dog. A dog's house is a kennel. Spirit had it right.

When my friends arrived, we went to the site and looked for the tree with the tape that Debbie had described. To our amazement, it was there with green and white hazard-type tape tied around it, not twenty yards away from the site I was about to excavate. Needless to say, my friends were very impressed with the messages from Spirit, but also very nervous.

I was certain I was on the right track and felt both excited and sad at the prospect of finding something that would lead to the discovery of another victim of Fred West's.

It took me four visits to dig down the 4ft into the hole, which was part of an old badger set. Little tunnels of the set were opening up as I dug. I reached the depth of 4ft, but all I found was a Lilt drinks can. I was disappointed – all that hard work for nothing!

It didn't make sense. Why would anyone dig a hole that big and fill it in if they hadn't buried anything?

I asked an ex-Forestry Commission man who had worked there in the seventies if the Forestry Commission would have dug into the sets – perhaps to gas the badgers.

He said, 'No.'

I asked him if badger baiters would have dug a hole that big to retrieve a dog.

Again, he answered, 'No.'

I gave it a lot of thought and came up with three possible options:

1) I had not dug deeply enough.
2) There had been something buried, but it had been removed.
3) The badgers had dragged whatever was buried there further into the set and could have, possibly, eaten it.

I went back to see Debbie and she said I should have gone deeper into the badgers' set.

Of course, I had broken the law in my search but it seemed irrelevant when it came to possibly finding a victim. The young man who had shown me the dig site had informed the police about the hole in 1994, but the police did not search it.

If the police didn't have the time or the funds to dig it up, I thought, someone had to do it. I also found a large car or lorry battery nearby, and remembered reading in one of the books that Fred West had poured battery acid into Rena's grave. I really felt that I should have kept going.

I tried to find the man who had seen the Monopoly money, but neither the police nor the *Citizen* newspaper that covered his story could tell me anything. If I could find this man and he confirmed it was near the dig site, I wouldn't think twice about digging until I found something.

I had found a partner in my search for further victims of the Wests in John Packer from the West Midlands. John had seen an article I'd had published in a newspaper about the messages I'd received from Spirit. He got in touch and we met up. John had done a lot of research of his own into the West murders and he, too, hoped to find other victims of the Wests.

We decided to go to Berkley Mill. Fred West was said to have confessed to his son, Stephen West, that he had done some terrible things there back in the sixties and seventies when it was not in use. In 1994, the police had visited the now-working flour mill, but no real search was made there. The owner had refused to let any members of the media into the buildings – but that didn't stop us!

John and I took two mediums with us on our visit. I will call them Peter and Jan. Jan stayed outside while we took Peter inside with us. Masquerading as historians, we told the manager that we were interested in old buildings and asked if we could take a look around. She said we could, as long as we didn't get in the way of the machinery. Unhindered by the manager's presence, as she was busy in her office, we wandered around the big old building, taking photos and videoing.

Peter did some dowsing and pointed to a place at the bottom of a wall, telling me that he believed there were two bodies buried under of the walls in the building at the rear of the mill, which was full of stage props from a pantomime set.

There was a length of rope tied up hanging from one of the beams. This room also had a bricked up stonewall that would have been an opening in to another room beyond it, which we couldn't get into.

Just outside this room, on our way back into the working part of the mill, we spotted a trap door. This led us to believe that there was a cellar running under the building. John was about to lift the trap door up when we were disturbed, so we didn't get a chance to look inside of it.

We looked in the outer buildings; behind the building there was a tall red-brick chimney. It looked like it hadn't been used for many years. There was also a disused, rotting two-berth caravan right outside the back of the room we had been in and a bricked-up doorway.

After having a good look around, we went back to our cars and found Jan, who was visibly shaken. She pointed to the same spot that Peter had indicated and said, 'There are two bodies buried there. They have no heads with them.'

We went to a coffee shop to discuss what the mediums had picked up. Jan was reluctant to tell me about it, as she was afraid I wouldn't be able to cope with what she had to tell us, but I insisted I could cope with whatever it was so she went on. 'This was Fred's place, only Fred came here. He would bring girls back here to use for himself. He would hang them up and leave them cold and naked and starve them. They were chilled to the bone. When they were completely disorientated, he would take them somewhere else for others to use.

'He did not kill them here, but brought their bodies back here to dispose of them. He worked, stripped to the waist, dismembering their bodies.

'There is a package somewhere; he has disposed of it in water, in a sluice. It could be an old film or video.'

Jan continued, 'There is more, but I don't wish to talk about it; it's too gruesome!'

A few weeks later, John and I, having heard more messages from Jan and Peter's friends, decided to go back to the flour mill unannounced to see what we could find. It was a bank holiday; the mill was closed, so we wandered around outside the building.

We were armed with a spade and dug up an indentation we had seen in a nearby sluice but found nothing. John looked through the old chimney stack and found an empty package in the shape of a book or video. It had brown parcel tape wrapped around and around it. Parcel tape like the tape Fred had used on his other victims and me!

I truly believe that if the police were to search through the mill then they would find more bodies, but they have no funding. As far as they are concerned, they had their man and now that he's dead and his partner in crime is in prison for life, they have no grounds to apply for funding to search the mill – plus, of course, the mill is still in use.

One day the mill will close down again. Hopefully, developers will move in to build on the land and they will find the remainder of Fred West's victims. God bless their souls. And if it's in my lifetime, I will be there too.

30

LESSONS LEARNED

TODAY I AM a very different person to the one I was before I discovered I was a survivor. I know we all go through different stages at different ages, but it has taken me till this year to realise we are what we want to be. Our lives are what we make of them. And only we, ourselves, are truly responsible for our actions and thoughts.

I believe that what we send out is returned to us. Life was a bitch to me because I had been a bitch to others, but I survived! I have also realised that the inner voice, which I chose to ignore every time it spoke, was my 'guardian angel' trying to protect me, but I was rebelling against it because I rebelled against anything and anyone who told me what to do.

My stepfather, Alf, had started out with good intentions of being a loving, supportive father to me, yet I rebelled against him, thinking that he had driven my real dad away. That is what

I thought as a child at the age of four, and I carried that thought with me through the years. As I got older, I convinced myself that it was true because the alternative was too painful to face. In my heart, I always knew that it was my real dad who had abandoned me, rejecting my brother Phillip and I.

Phillip, unlike me, faced up to the fact and got on with his life. He appreciated Alf for all he had done for us, while I made life hell for Alf, throwing his love back in his face till he gave up on me. I believe this is why Phillip despised me so much when I was younger.

While I was writing this book, I realised there were times when even Phillip showed his love for me and I was blind to it. Once when, as a fifteen-year-old, I was caught kissing a friend's ex-boyfriend, Phillip came to my rescue when things turned nasty. This girl was a bully and often beat up other girls, but she had befriended me for some reason. I had betrayed her friendship and she wanted revenge, so she tried to get me into a car to drag me off for a beating. As she threw me into the car I struggled, so she slammed the car door on my legs. I was lucky they were not broken.

Another friend, Julie, went running off to get help and Phillip and some of his mates came running up the road to help me. When my attacker saw that she and her two male accomplices were outnumbered, she drove off, but not before ripping my hair out and punching me. I was on the pavement, unconscious and covered in blood when Phillip reached me. Phillip carried me home that day. When Mum saw us, she said that she was certain I must be dead and she never wanted to see me like that again.

Another time, just after the Wests had attacked me, Phillip

once again showed that he cared. Phillip and some of his mates had gone to 25 Cromwell Street to give Fred West a kicking, but he did not answer the door to them. So they hung around waiting for him, shouting to Fred to come out and face them, calling him a 'rapist' and telling him what they were going to do with him. The police were called and the lads were moved on. I didn't know anything about this until the police came to the house to see Phillip and give him a warning.

I only ever seemed to remember the bad things that had happened between Phillip and me, never the good. We may have had our fights, but when I needed him he was there for me. Only now can I see it. Since leaving home, we have got along much better and I always remember to send him a birthday card; it's my way of showing him that I do love him. We're not very good at showing physical affection towards each other as yet, but that is something that I hope will come in time.

I've also learned, and finally accepted, that as a child I was very aware of my sexuality. I believe all children are sexual creatures and children do experiment with each other. It is not appropriate behaviour, but it is natural. Very often, when children are caught behaving in this way, they are severely reprimanded for the compromising position they are found in by the person who finds them. (Usually the parent of one of the children.) That person is usually so shocked that they tell the child that they are bad and disgusting and that what they are doing is dirty – that *they* are dirty.

This sets off the feelings of guilt and shame in the children that haunts some of them for the rest of their lives. Some of them get over it; some, like myself, do not and we carry it with us throughout our lives, making us feel ashamed of ourselves and ashamed of enjoying sex, even in a long-term, loving relationship.

It was these feeling of shame I carried that made me feel I was no good, that is was disgusting and dirty. These feelings led me into too many sexual encounters. I was a sexual being and others saw it in me. They also saw I was lonely and vulnerable and in need of physical love. It showed in the way I behaved, in my appearance and in my body language.

All my life I had confused sex with love. I was searching for the love of a man and my sexuality was my way of attracting a man. And because sex was my bartering tool to get the love I so much needed, I ended up being rejected again and again. It wasn't love I was getting, it was sex, but I felt better about myself when I called it love. I was in denial once again because the alternative was too painful to bear.

When the Wests were arrested in 1994, all the feelings of shame and guilt I had in my teens came back to trouble me with a vengeance. The day I heard the first news report about the Wests changed me. I could not stand for Ian to touch me. I felt he was just using me. Sex became strained and less frequent, as each time I felt more and more uptight about it. I felt guilty when I enjoyed it. I couldn't relax or show Ian the love I felt for him.

I was angry about these feelings I had allowed to surface and didn't know how to help myself. I did what I usually did — blamed everyone else for my unhappiness when really it was my old feelings of self-hate that were surfacing.

I accused Ian of not being supportive enough when I was going through the trial. Yet it was me who had told him I didn't want him there. I became more and more suspicious of Ian; the more he tried to show me love, the more I rejected him. I tried to drive him away before he could hurt me like my real dad had by leaving me.

In May 2000, I decided to find my dad, but I'd left it too late and I got a surprise: I discovered he had died in the February of that year. His family was shocked when they were told he had two other children. Some family members were mortified that he could have kept such a thing a secret for so long, but they accepted me. Others chose not to believe it. But through it all I have now got two uncles that have welcomed me into their families; an aunt who has accepted that I am her brother's daughter, but would like me to stay a secret; and a half-brother that cannot come to terms with the new situation, which I can completely understand. And I've a half-sister, Helen, who was at first very hurt and shocked by the revelation, but seems to have come to terms with the fact that she has an elder sister and brother. Since then she and I have met and talked. We send each other birthday and Christmas presents and chat now and then on the phone and I feel a great deal of affection towards her.

I have learned that many people live their lives to please others. I believe my dad knew it would hurt his family back in Ireland that he had two children out of wedlock. He was revered by his family and was seen to be a devout Catholic, a good man.

I think he was a good man and that he knew he could not marry my mum because he knew it was not a marriage that would last. My mum was still a free spirit and it had cost her his love and trust.

I needed time to find out what I wanted from life and which

things were important to me. In September 1999, I took a risk and separated from Ian for sixteen months. We had drifted apart so much since we had got married, and even before that, since the West case had come up. We never did anything together as a couple; he always needed someone else with us if we went anywhere. It got to the point that we only went out separately and had developed different interests; we had nothing in common except that we both loved our children. I wanted to find out if we were together because we loved each other or because we had children together.

We still saw each other every day because Ian had to babysit while I worked evenings, but I did whatever I wanted to, while he preferred to stay in. I joined a 'development circle' with Debbie and five other people from Monmouth Spiritualist Church and began to get a better understanding of myself and others, including Ian.

I went away on a few weekends to Butlins with my single friends and had a good time. And although the opportunity was there to be with other attractive men, I didn't bother. I found out that Ian was the only one I wanted to be with. I had always thought that if we separated it would be Ian that went off with someone else, but he didn't either.

Although I was twice his age, it was me that he found attractive and it was me he loved. He didn't want anyone else, I didn't want anyone else, so we got back together in January 2001. It has not been easy for either of us, as we have had to accept that we are two very different people. We have our different needs and different outlooks on life, which we have both come to accept and respect. We have both learned that we have to compromise to get the best out of our relationship and to build the best future for our children. Things are not always perfect between Ian and I; we both lose our tempers from time to time. But we don't let it get us down and we're still working on it.

I'm learning to love myself now and how to show love to my family and strangers alike. I have decided to give up my well-paid job at Xerox and do more reiki healing. I intend to train as a drugs counsellor so I can do my bit towards helping those who are tormented by their addiction. And I am already working on a book about my spiritual experiences and how they have helped to make my life worth living.

I always thought I was the 'perpetual victim'. Now I know I am not. I survived when others perished and for that I am truly grateful. I have made a promise to Rena Costello, Ann McFall, Charmaine West, Linda Gough, Carol Ann Cooper, Lucy Partington, Therese Siegenthaler, Shirley Hubbard, Juanita Mott, Shirley Robinson, Alison Chambers and Heather West, that I will do something positive with my life. I could not prevent their deaths, but I will help to prevent the death of others.

I know that they are all happy in spirit and I send out love to them every day, and as I write these words I feel them around me, returning that love tenfold. God bless you all.

EPILOGUE

IT'S TAKEN ME ten years to complete this book. This has been my therapy and now I can let go of the past and move on. My life has changed, I have changed. I have grown, which has meant I have had to leave some people behind.

I have nothing in common with most of my old friends; we're on different pathways. I'm hungry to learn, I want to travel, I want to experience life now, not just drift through it aimlessly waiting for the weekend and a good piss-up, a snort or a joint. I have to make decisions about what I want, and not let anyone hold me back. If I'm happy I can make life for my children and family happy. I've spent enough time pleasing others; it's time to please myself now. And no, I don't think I'm being a bitch. I think I'm being good to myself because I deserve it.

I leave you with something pragmatic and profound: life's a bitch and then you survive.